*bec...*

# MOTH

# change

# EMMASARA
# MCMILLION

McMillion & Co. Publishing
PO BOX 502
Van Horn, TX 79855
ISBN- 978-1-7346361-8-5

**Cover Design- Bijou & Davae McMillion**
**Cover Photographer- Erick Robinson**
**Editor- Bijou McMillion**
**Contributor- Stella Winingham**
**Format- Nile McMillion**
**Illustrator-Davae McMillion**

Unless otherwise indicated, all Scripture is taken from: New King James Version (NKJV). Scripture taken from the New King James Version®. Copyright © 1982 by Thomas Nelson. Used by permission. All rights reserved. King James Version (KJV). Public Domain

# Book Reviews

*"If you are single, married, have children or expecting to have children then this is A MUST READ! I'm married with 7 children plus 2 bonus babies from marriage, so I have 9 chldren. I recently went through a period of feeling discouraged and losing hope. I finally opened up my MOC book, and INSTANTLY she touched my heart! I was reminded who I Am and whose I AM! I was reminded I am royalty even though most days I didn't feel it! When I got the revelation, my Father is a King and I've been adopted into the royal family, I immediately sat up and held my head high! Now it was time to start making changes with myself and my household! This was the beginning of change! If you are looking for guidance and transparency, this book has it all!*
"-Keyotta Collins, Mama to 9

*"Emma Sara is full of wisdom. I love the way she breaks down every single topic along with the Word of God. As if she speaking directly to me. You can tell that God truly inspired her to write this book for us. I already feel empowered!! Thank You Emma Sara! You truly are the mother of change."*
— Melissa, empowered mom

"This book will grab your attention. It is like EmmaSara is my personal coach or mentor. Ok so what I absolutely love about this book is I don't feel defeated. I feel like I can make changes in my home and it's not too late. I am so encouraged." – Kellie Jackson, teacher & mom.

# Preface

When people find out that I have eight kids, it's natural for them to assume I probably always wanted to have a big family. However, that couldn't be further from the truth. As a young adult, I never wanted to have children because I thought this world was too evil. Besides, I didn't think I would have the patience for kids, and I know some of my family members wondered the same.

However, God has a sense of humor and a way of...

*Turning our world upside down*

*to make our life right side up.*

So, I want to acknowledge Him first. If it were not for the wisdom and grace of God in my life, I would not have the good fruit that I see abounding in my kids. If it wasn't for Him humbling me over and over, I might not be the parent I am today. My eight kids are not only a joy to me, but they are also enjoyable for others to be around, and the credit goes to practicing Godly principles raising them. I learned from the best: The Holy Spirit and the Bible, mixed with experience from the school of hard knocks.

I would also like to acknowledge my kids, who have been open to the constant, consistent, intentional parenting methods they have experienced throughout their lives. It's because of their grace and constant forgiveness that I can write this book. I said I was consistent, but I didn't say I was perfect or without fault. When I think about it, I don't know if I have ever met a perfect parent. I know some parents can seem flawless, but we all have room to grow. So, I am eternally grateful for my husband's patience while I experience life refinement and for his support in the cause of raising world-changers. I am also thankful for my children who have matured alongside me in personal development.

Finally, I would also like to acknowledge my mom, who was only fourteen when she had me. She broke every mold and chain that she could to provide the best for me. She was intentional about safety and protected me even as a teen mother. I would also like to recognize my dad for showing me what loyalty and dedication look like in action. Because of them both, I learned how to live a life of accountability without excuse! Thanks, Mom and Dad!

# It's Time for Change!

"I am sorry, but your child didn't make it..."

It's the awful news too many moms hear today. No mama thinks it will be her child, but the truth is that the stats are rising.

o Suicide is now the leading cause of death for children ages 10 to 14 in Ohio, and it's the leading cause of death for young people, from the ages of 15 to 34.[15]
o School bullying is becoming deadly.
o School shootings are on the rise.

These high stats leave the nation asking, *Why is this happening?* I believe that working to solve these critical issues begins within the home.

Maybe you have thought, *how can I safeguard my kids better? How can I strengthen my home and family relations? Or, how can I, as a mother, battle for my kids no matter how old they are?*

If you have ever had a caution in your spirit to protect your children, you landed in the right spot.

In the following pages, you will gain **powerful strategies** to:

1. Protect your kids.
2. Reduce conflicts.
3. Safeguard your home spiritually.
4. Gain respect from your children.
5. Break off broken mindsets.
6. Increase cooperation.
7. Raise kids who honor God.
8. Identify how the enemy works to destroy the family home.

Mama, I know that you desire to protect your children and your relationship with them, and I am here to help.

I understand that a mom's life is not for the faint-hearted. So I want to thank you for your dedication to pursuing growth for your family. I also want to welcome you to the Mother of Change Movement! I believe that moms are the unsung heroes of our nation. I am sure there are days you feel empowered and ready to take on the world, yet there may be times that you feel guilty because you wish you could be doing more or better. Today, I want you to be encouraged and excited about the journey that lies ahead! Get ready to experience life change. Let God's grace empower you to break off every chain that has held you back from accomplishing all you are called to do as a mom and woman of God! Set aside time to show up daily and dive into this book.

I guarantee that if you are truly ready for change, by the time you complete this book, you will feel empowered to step into your role as a Warrior Mom and Mother of Change!

✓ Be prepared to be challenged!
✓ Be prepared to change!
✓ Be prepared to grow!

Parenting: no one said that it would be easy, but it's worth it!

# Table of Contents

## The Warfare Mom 139

## Mom Manual 177

## World Changer Mom 231

# Start Here

Mama, I wrote this book with a legacy in mind. So, I believe that it will become your mom-manual for generations. Since life is always evolving and changing, there needs to be an anchor within the framework of a family home. Without one, you risk roaming aimlessly. The Mother of Change Strategy will provide strong anchor points for your family structure so that you will be unmovable in the storms of life.

This training manual was written for the moms in the trenches. It was written for you. It doesn't matter how old your kids are, whether they are toddlers or twenty years old, there is something here for you. Mama, I know you have a lot on your schedule, and you have your family to tend to, so I broke up areas for you to work on bit by bit if you have to.

If you are a studier, I included scripture references for personal study. Although I love digging into the Word, this is not written in a theological dissertation style. If I did, this book might sit on a shelf gathering dust for moms who are hungry for immediate family strategies.

I admit I am one of those moms who like references, so I made sure to include those in the back of the book for the deep studiers. The bottom line is that I am writing as a mom to moms. I do cover a lot of topics, and it might feel like you're trying to take a drink out of fire hydrant if you decide to consume it all at once. To make stepping into becoming a Mother of Change a more straightforward process, I broke up the book into three sections.

**Once you complete Section One which is focused on family strategy, you can celebrate!** Consider it graduation from M.O.C. Training. It's like graduating from high school. You fulfilled all the requirements you need to enter the next stage of life. College is optional but so beneficial to further your education. Sections Two and Three are like those upper-level classes: helpful, but they can be tackled after you get your house in order. If you are need of a lot of home adjustments, focus on getting up to speed with Section One first. I included sections Two and Three because I get a lot of questions on the section topics. *Ultimately, I feel like adding them to your family culture is vital to building a powerful legacy for God and our nation.*

My desire is for you to begin this journey with prayer. Ask God to help you uncover the areas that need to be addressed immediately within your home. The beauty of the Mother of Change Strategy is that it's possible to experience victories quickly! How great is that?

I am not trying to go so deep that I lose you in the process. I want to give you food for thought and inspire you to experience family life in a new way.

# *You can create change within your home for the glory of God.*

Remember:

1. Even little changes are changes.
2. Every step forward is progress.
3. Every habit broken is a victory won!

If you are wondering if I have more than mom wisdom, I do. My professional background includes being a former director of a women's and children's shelter that I managed for over two years. During that time, I wrote the client recovery curriculum, and I also took additional substance abuse and relational training. I have extensive experience working with adopted children. Currently, I am a family strategist consultant. Honestly, I feel my best experience comes from being a mama of eight kids, ages one to twenty years old. Some of our best life lessons came from what felt like a very long season living in a 235 square-feet RV from May 2014 to February 2019. To add to that adventure, my husband lost his entire income almost overnight during that time. For months we were living below a poverty-level income. Times were rough. Let's just say our family knows what it's like to live in lack and with plenty. We have had quite a journey, but we made it through victorious!

My kids are not perfect, so over the years, my focus has been to build Godly character in them. The fruit is shown in their lives as they are pleasant to be around, wise, discerning, creative, helpful, lovable, friendly, and they love God. My four teens are entrepreneurs who desire to become the change our world needs.

If you are here to grow as a parent and as a woman of God, you're in the right place. You will be equipped to train, conquer, battle, and protect your children!  Read over a chapter and create a weekly goal for yourself based upon the chapter strategy or insight. Start with self-reflection and then focus on how you can implement each section's lesson to your parenting style.

Change for the better is on the horizon!

Are you ready? Let's go

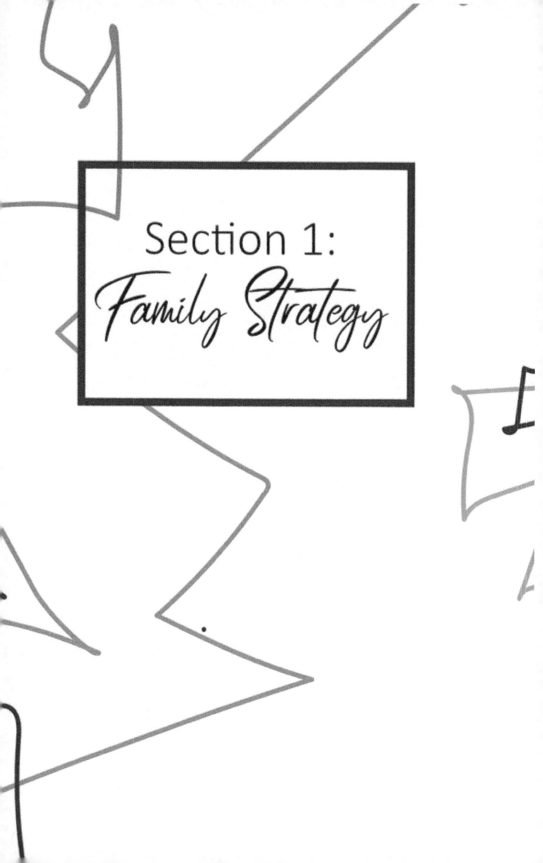

# Section 1:
## Family Strategy

# Chapter 1

## Mom Talk

# You Deserve Honor

Mama, you were created by God to magnify His glory and His splendor. So, let's pave this journey by establishing an understanding of who we are as daughters of God. Before we enter this topic, you need to understand your heavenly worth.

There are two main reasons why you deserve honor:

1. God has established an order for the home, and it includes kids honoring, respecting, and submitting to their parents.
2. You are the daughter of a King, and since Jesus is the King of Kings, as His daughter, that makes you royalty, which means you deserve honor.

If we, as mothers, lose sight of those two truths, we can easily forget the authority we have within our home. If we don't require honor from our kids, then our house will be out of order. Remember, it's God's will to both bless and establish you as a mother with a high calling. The high calling is to raise children of light, children of God. So, walk with your head held high within your home. Just envision all the opulence and grandeur that surrounds the office of royalty. Americans don't live with a monarchy, but we can still get a peek into a royal lifestyle by observing Meghan Markle,

Britain's newest princess. With all the royal news, this sparked my curiosity about a literal royal lifestyle, so my girls and I looked into what living as royalty requires. We found out there is a list of standards that they are expected to uphold in public. Not only do they have a list of personal boundaries they must keep, but there is also structure and rules about how the general public must treat and socialize with them. That's right; you can't just go up and shake the queen's hand or hug a princess. So take note, studying the royal system can be instructive.

I have eight kids, and I have taught them to view me as both the queen and princess of our home, which has produced both loyalty and respect. My kids can't treat me as a peer, and they can't try to rule over me. As a matter of fact, according to the Bible, children are to honor their parents.

*Honor your Father and your mother, as the LORD your God has commanded you, that your days may be long, and that it may be well with you in the land which the LORD your God is giving you. (Deut. 5:16)*

Mama remember you are worthy of being treated with respect and honor!

*Children, obey your parents in the Lord, for this is right. "Honor your father and mother," which is the first commandment with promise: "that it may be well with you and you may live long on the earth. (Eph. 6:1-3)*

Even though some days you may not feel worthy, remember your value is set in heaven and comes from God. He establishes your worth because you are His creation, and His Word states you are worthy of respect from your children.

**If you are ready to turn the tide in your home:**

Don't allow backtalk.

1. Don't allow your kids to take advantage of you.
2. Instead, encourage them to do acts of service for you without feeling guilty. My sons love to spoil me. They even argue about who will give me a foot massage! Their acts of service bless me so much.
3. Require them to honor you in word and deed.

Consider this as a beautiful new season to grow. Get your heart and mind prepared to practice new habits in your home. Also, each time you sit down to open this book, I will suggest again to start with prayer. Ask the Holy Spirit to help you absorb what you need for personal development - both as a mother and a woman of God. Then, if you are struggling, you will be strengthened. If you are excelling, you will execute with more precision! Earlier I had you envision living like royalty. Now envision laying down your royal attire for a moment to get changed into training attire. Why? Because you are about to enter a training zone, a place where moms regain the power to raise children that will change the world!

Be prepared to learn how to become a Mother of Change and operate in the empowerment of motherhood.

# Mom Confidence

Mama, we have talked about the importance of receiving honor, but we also need to talk about *"mom confidence."* It's common for moms to lack self-confidence. If this is an area you struggle with, your kids will feed off your deficit of self-esteem, and many times they will take advantage of the lack. As a matter of fact, as I was writing this chapter, my phone beeped, and it was a prayer request from a friend. She was struggling with self-doubt in her parenting. She was frustrated that her efforts weren't producing the right fruit in her kids. Thoughts were filling her mind like, "I can't wait until the kids are out of the house because I don't know if I am qualified to do a good job."

She was pouring out her heart in a vulnerable way to seek counsel and prayer. So, I responded, "Ask Yahweh for 'mom confidence!'" Many times, we can have a level of surety in certain areas of life but lack confidence in how to lead our kids. Sometimes we need assurance in how to train them up. This deficiency is birthed from fear, which leads to double-mindedness. We start to question our ability to parent correctly, and so we begin to give up and give in.

**Annihilate wavering self-trust by proclaiming over yourself:**

1. I am sure of myself.
2. I am confident in my decisions.
3. I do hear from God.

4. I deserve to be respected by my children.

Write down these plus more "mom confidence" statements and make them part of your life affirmations when you feel yourself wavering or lacking self-assurance.

My friend texted me back later and was comforted because my suggestion was in alignment with her morning prayer for direction, which reminded me that mom confidence is birthed from a pure place, not a perfect place. You don't have to understand things 100 percent to pursue a path of righteousness; choose to set a lifestyle in motion that is in pursuit of glorifying God as you are learning.

If you lack spiritual confidence, it's likely because you haven't developed strong lifestyle convictions for yourself. Fear is a common deterrent in developing both personal and lifestyle surety. You can't operate with assertiveness if you're riddled with fear. The most common fear-factor is making the wrong decision. If you don't want to sabotage your mom-mission, don't be lead by it; it's a thief of security!

I have made a lot of parenting mistakes for sure.

However, one thing I did right was I learned to trust God for daily guidance. In doing so, I managed to raise my kids with satisfaction. In other words, I am content with the parenting experience. I'm at peace with how my kids are growing up. I have trusted that God granted me the authority and wisdom I needed to protect my kids and raise them according to the Bible.

As daughters of God, we have the power to influence our kids and future generations to come! Are you hungering for it? Somewhere in life, I heard the statement, "don't fear failure, but be terrified of regret." I got it; we should avoid making decisions that will lead to regret. However, being terrified of anything is emotionally unhealthy, so I wasn't about to internalize the terrified part.

Instead, I chose to be an intentional parent, spending the last twenty years of parenting focused on having the least amount of regret as possible. Every step of the way, I acknowledged that God qualified me to raise a generation of children that would bring hope to this world.

Mama, if you are reading this book, please, acknowledge that God has qualified you to do the same.

# Choose boldness + confidence

Let boldness and confidence be the lenses you choose to view life through.

Become "mom confident," which I define as leading your kids with certainty, believing that the decisions you make are right for the moment.

# *I Lead my kids with certainty, believing my decisions are right for the moment.*

Did you hear that? I didn't say a lifetime, but a moment.

You can have a long-lasting, generational focus with the understanding that *confidence is established in the **now moments** of life.* I try to stay focused on hearing God's word for the moment. Why is this so important? Because life ebbs and flows and what's okay yesterday, may not be okay today and vice versa.

# *Be flexible to hear God's voice for the day.*

Some moms make cold hard rules, and they box themselves in. They become legalistic, or worse; they become judgmental of others. So, you won't hear me counsel a mom to become dogmatic. I personally find that type of attitude unloving and likened to the Pharisees' behavior. They were the religious teachers of their time. They knew the Torah or the Law of God, yet their hearts were far from him. They were caught up with the rules and missed the heart of God. In my early years of parenting, the

Lord dealt with me in this area. Let's just say obedience is better than sacrifice.

So, what does mom confidence look like in action?

It's the development of very noble character traits that come from truly desiring God's best for you and your children. This means trusting His perfect will for your household. Confidence is established by having grace for yourself! Accept that you will make mistakes and be okay with that! Be transparent with your kids. When you feel the Lord is leading you somewhere else or into deeper waters of faith, share that insight with your kids and involve them in the process. We have made so many changes in our family dynamic over the years, but thankfully this didn't appear to be double-mindedness or shaky ground to our kids. Instead, we were able to make a lot of course corrections and still stay completely rooted and grounded in our faith. Most importantly, our kids have trusted the deviations we have made in our daily family life. I have taught them that our focus is to remain close to God's plan for our lives, which means lifestyle changes are inevitable as we remain open to the voice of the Spirit of the Lord. Having your children's total trust is one of the most rewarding gifts you can experience as a parent.

Are you ready to have real mom confidence? First, kick the fear of failing to the curb by following step one. Then follow the rest of these steps:

1. **Have grace for yourself** because you will experience failures. Yes, I said it, you will fail. Every human being will experience momentary failures in life. It's a part of

the journey. But, remember that just because you failed doesn't make you a failure. Dust yourself off and get back up!

2. **Repent** to Yahweh and your kids. To repent is defined as showing sincere regret or remorse. In other words, tell your kids and God, you are sorry. Most importantly, repentance is also defined as completely turning away from a sin you previously committed.

3. **Keep moving toward God's best** for your family. Don't fall into depression, guilt, or sabotage.

4. **Be transparent** in the lessons and chastisements you get from the Lord. Don't hide your mistakes! Share them with your family and grow past them!

5. **Study the Word** to know how to live. Read a Proverb a day to keep a bad attitude away. Not only will you learn about the foolish versus the wise, but you will also find out about how to conduct your life according to the Bible in just one chapter a day. A good reading schedule is to match the chapter with the day. If it's the first day of the month, read chapter one. Our family followed that pattern for years, and I can say it never got boring, and there was always a new lesson for the day.

6. **Don't be moved** from your decisions that are based upon godly convictions. People can have their point of view. Don't be bullied into caving into popular opinion! Remember to stand strong in your decisions, say what you mean, and mean what you say.

7. **Follow-through.** Don't say something unless you plan to stick to your word.

If you are continually changing your mind because you are riddled with fear or guilt, this will not produce good fruit in your house. However, if God tells you to course correct or you read something in the Bible that causes your heart to be moved, discuss it with your family and get them on board through prayer and dialog. In other words, let them feel included in the transition. Let them form a conviction of their own after you took the time to work it out with them. Including them allows them to develop their own thoughts so they can take ownership of the changes made.

I'm not a parent that tries to shove views down my kids' throat. Unfortunately, there are strict parents who give orders without proper communication, and that is rarely fruitful. Being intentional is the solution. I invite my kids to a place where they take ownership of lifestyle decisions. It's a communication process that I combine with prayer and trusting God.

So now it's time for you to enter into prayer for you and your husband, (or future husband) pray that you would be united in how you raise your kids. If you are single, ask for empowerment to do hard things and for unity within your household.

*Just because you failed,*
*doesn,t make you a failure.*

# Accountability

How many times have you told your child to throw out the trash or do some other daily chores only to have them forget? How many times do they need to be told to remember? I have yet to meet a mom that has reported her child executes 100 percent of every task they are given without a reminder. Okay, so if you are the first parent with a different report, please write me and let me know so I can make a note, and, yes, I really want to know! It would give me hope that it is indeed possible! Yet the truth is kids will make mistakes and they will forget. So, why, dear mama, do we expect perfection from our kids as if it were possible? Stop and ponder that for a bit. Go ahead, you can even stop and pause to ask God to reveal areas to work on in your life. Now can we be real with each other? How many times has God asked you to do something or moved you to complete something or change an attitude, and you listened the first time? I bet you thought this chapter was going to be focused on keeping kids accountable, and it is to some degree, but I am asking you to focus on personal accountability first.

---

*So then each of us shall give account of himself to God. (Romans 14:12)*

---

Accountability is taking responsibility for our actions or inaction. It's an important element in every believer's life because we will each give an account to God on the last day, and we will be held responsible for our life choices. So this is something you can't ignore.

As moms, we will inevitably suffer the frustration of a child who has not obeyed an instruction. Sometimes they choose to disobey, and other times they just honestly forget. Have you ever responded either way when God told you to do something? I think Yahweh has grace when we forget, but what about when we willfully disobey?

My point is this: is it fair to desire something from our kids that we are not first giving to God, which is our immediate, long-lasting obedience? *Before concentrating on your kid's obedience level, I am calling on you to take a personal inventory of any lack of obedience in your life.*

### Five steps to take a self-inventory:

1. Ask God to reveal any disobedience in your life.
2. Write down any hypocritical behavior.
3. Ask your kids to name one behavior you can improve upon as a mom. Make sure you provide a safe place for them to be honest. In other words, don't get upset by what they share. Don't show negative emotion and thank them for their honesty.
4. Take all your findings and journal them, so you don't forget.
5. Repent to God and your children. Then FORGIVE yourself.

Then you will be empowered to understand how to respond to your children's lack of follow-through. Scripture says to first take the plank out of our own eye before trying to remove the speck in someone else's eye.

---

*Or how can you say to your brother, 'Let me remove the speck from your eye'; and look, a plank is in your own eye? Hypocrite! First remove the plank from your own eye, and then you will see clearly to remove the speck from your brother's eye.*
*(Mat. 7:3-5)*

---

This means we (and I emphasize "we") can get busy calling out the tiny things our children do and ignore the fact that the Father sees us exhibiting the same behavior. Ouch! I know this may hit close to home. However, no one said it would be easy parenting, but it's worth the challenge to grow! Even I am shaking in my boots in a reverential kind of way as I write! I must remind myself of this lesson often because it can be easy to forget. We have to keep going back to the basics sometimes. This morning during my Bible reading time, I came across this passage of a brother and sister complaining about    their brother and his new bride because of her ethnicity.:

---

*So the anger of the L*ORD *was aroused against them, and He departed. And when the cloud departed from above the tabernacle, suddenly Miriam became leprous, as white as snow. Then Aaron turned toward Miriam, and there she was, a leper. So Aaron said to Moses, "Oh, my lord! Please do not lay this sin on us, in which we have done foolishly and* *in which we have sinned. Please do not let her be as one dead, whose flesh is half consumed when he comes out of his mother's womb!" (Numb. 12)*

---

Did you notice how Aaron  cried out to the LORD for his sister? He also acknowledged that he and his sister acted foolishly.

---

*Then the Lord said to Moses, "If her Father had but spit in her face, would she not be shamed seven days? Let her be shut[f] out of the camp seven days, and afterward she may be received again." So Miriam was shut out of the camp seven days, and the people did not journey till*
*Miriam was brought in again. (Num. 12)*

---

I found myself studying this passage, and I pondered the cause of the Lord's anger. It was apparent that Miriam was partaking in unsavory talk with her brother Aaron and was acting with pride. Yet Moses was noted as being one of the humblest men on earth. So here she was calling out Moses on his choice of bride while positioning herself as equal to Moses regarding having favor with Yahweh. Clearly, she had her own heart issues to deal with, but instead, she was concentrating on the "speck" she thought she saw in her brother's eye before pulling the "plank" of pride and prejudice out of her own eye. How did Yahweh deal with this? He gave a steep consequence and was moved to holy anger. Eventually, He did have grace and allowed Miriam to return to the camp after being removed for seven days. When I read passages like this, I take note that the Father has emotions of elation and frustration, just like we do as parents. It's at that point I am moved to a place of self-accountability.

At that moment, I self-reflect and seek my Daddy, my Abba.

**It's the perfect time to ask God these two questions:**

1. How have I offended You?
2. How have I disobeyed You either willfully or mindlessly?

This time spent in prayer is when we get right with God.

Each time I pray this kind of prayer, He is so good to show me what I need to repent, and course-correct from.

The flesh's response is to excuse or overlook personal sin by letting a kid's actions slide because we are not keeping up to par ourselves, but as I said, that would be the flesh. The spiritual response is to stop and take accountability for how we are falling short and missing the mark. This allows us to repent and turn from our poor behavior and have a proper heart to correct our children correctly. There is a certain empowerment given to parents that humble themselves when they remain in accountability to God.

I'm a woman who makes mistakes constantly, but I repent often. No, I am not trying to take advantage of grace. Instead, it's about acknowledging my daily need for the Savior. It's about dying to the flesh daily. It makes me think of the analogy of a ship at sea. It could be easy for a ship to get off course since there are no roads in the water. So a ship's captain must be constantly aware of his location coordinates, meaning that continual course corrections are important.

Daily life is the same way. We need a navigation device to do this. Even if a captain can have excellent training and a vast understanding of the sea, that knowledge can only go so far without a navigation device. In the same way, we need to be in the Word every single day and pray for our path to be made clear by seeking which way we should go. Taking a daily personal moral inventory is so important for successful parenting.

Mama, would you take a moment to bow your head and pray?

Would you do some soul searching based upon the journal entries you made earlier from your self-inventory list?

Be ready for correction. Be ready for instruction. And, most importantly, be ready to tell the enemy to take a hike if he throws guilt and shame at you during this beautiful, vulnerable process. Remember, if God delights in it, then the enemy loathes it. Don't let him steal this intimate moment that will lead you into a stage of deep intense growth.

# Prayer

Father, please show me where I lack personal accountability. Reveal to me areas I have behaved like a hypocrite. Show me how to take better self-accountability so that I can lead my kids with a pure conscience. Show me where I can make improvements. In your name, Jesus. Amen

# Meltdown Mama

Are you a mama that has meltdowns? Do you find yourself making mistakes, only to stop and beat yourself up, which deflates your motivation and productivity? When something goes wrong, do you lose your momentum and all the plans and ideas you had to be productive come to a halt? Does a kid or spouse do something that rubs you the wrong way, and you immediately lose your cool? These reactions are all signs of an adult meltdown. As mamas, we know that kids can have them, but moms can too. If this sounds like you, then I want you to visualize that you are in a vehicle with your kids. Imagine that you are in a new town on your way to the store, when all of a sudden you turn down the wrong street. Imagine yourself getting flustered and pulling over. See yourself having a meltdown and thinking about how you messed up by turning down the wrong street. Imagine the kids are all in the seats just watching you have this meltdown. From the back seat, you can hear them saying, "Why are we stopped?" "Why don't we just get back on the road?"

They're right. It's no big deal; you just turned down the wrong street. You have a GPS, so it's not like you don't know where to go or how to get there. All you need to do is make a U-turn and get on the right street, and you will be at your destination in no time. Instead, you're pulled over with the whole family in the car watching you, while you are stuck on the side of the road by choice. Nothing is keeping you there except your decision to pull over and turn off the ignition. You never had to skip a beat. You could have just course-corrected without any snags or stops in your day. Sure, it may have taken a little longer to get to your destination because you took a detour. However, because you kept going, you will get there soon enough. Now every time you make a mistake, or you find yourself stuck emotionally, imagine yourself in the vehicle—stuck on the side of the road—and remind yourself how easy it is to get back on the road and head in the right direction.

Remember, meltdowns can happen because of any of the following reasons:

1. You don't want to be a failure.
2. You are too hard on yourself.
3. You are making a big deal of small issues.
4. You need to de-stress and take some self-care time.

During your moment of pause, this is also a good time to take personal inventory, as discussed earlier in the chapter on Accountability.

When you are willing to forgive yourself quickly, grace is enough to get you back on the road.

### How to take control of personal meltdowns quickly:

1. Dealing with kids- Get back on the road quickly by recognizing sometimes miscommunication is the issue and not disrespect. If this is the case, this means no one was trying to sabotage or be disobedient.

2. Dealing with self- Have a positive self-dialog. Talk yourself into responding with strength. Remind yourself; it's no big deal, just keep going, everything will be fine. It's not the end of the world. Plenty of people have it way worse. I should be grateful.

When you go on a road trip, you want to make sure you get there safely. You would never put your children in harm's way, so do your best not to destroy your relationship with them by being emotionally unstable. A driver who is on the side of the road having a meltdown, is emotionally unstable, even if for just a moment. GSo gather yourself and get back on the road! Remember, the mistake is not what's detrimental to our children; it' is how we handle it that can cause the worst damage. So show your kids that life's wrong turns don't have to be catastrophic events! Make your mistakes, have grace for yourself and others, course correct, and keep moving!

# Rehearse the Pain Mama

Have you ever been wronged in life? Who hasn't, right? Or, have you been deeply hurt? This exercise is for you! Just because you have been victimized doesn't mean you have to continue to be a victim! The enemy wants you to get stuck in mental pain, but you are here, and you can be strong! Retain your power by not rehearsing the pain, because every time you rehearse the pain, you allow yourself to be victimized repeatedly, and that is not okay. It was never okay. So, it's definitely not okay that the memory is still causing damage in your mind or relationships. Unfortunately, many women who have been traumatized go into an autopilot mode of despair when stress comes about. But you and I are capable of controlling our lives. So, take the wheel!

Maybe you haven't experienced deep trauma; instead, your issue is creating your own mental drama. Whatever the case, take every thought captive and bring it under subjection and obedience of Christ. Stop letting your mind control you! You must learn to control your thoughts.

I know it's easy to run through a situation repeatedly in your mind but stop it! Ask yourself:

- What does rehearsing the pain accomplish in my life?
- What kind of fruit has it produced?

- How has it benefited my kids and family? It probably hasn't, right?

It's time to stop uniting with broken thinking. Separate yourself from thoughts that bring despair, hurt, and suck motivation from your life!

*The following visualization will help you understand that your negative thoughts are not one with you.*

I want you to put your hand to your forehead and **swipe** it!

As you swipe it, visualize all the negative thoughts in your head being swiped out of your mind. Imagine any traumatic scenes in your life swiped off the screen of your mind. **Swipe** negative thoughts! I know if I walked into a room and found my kids watching a mentally damaging video, I would immediately stop it and swipe it off the screen to close it out. Why? Because it contains material that is not safe to watch! So stop playing unsafe scenes in your mind. We can experience mental damage just like they can.

If negative thoughts come up, *Take Action*:

1. <u>Swipe</u> the thought away.
2. **Visualize it leaving your mind.**
3. **Replace it with a positive thought** because every bad habit must be replaced with a good habit.

Now you have a visualization tool to help you understand how to separate your thoughts because they are not one with you. They are like inappropriate videos that need to be removed from your mind! Why would you allow something

48

to play in your home that satan delights in, whether it is music, movies, games, or whatever? Your thoughts are no different. Safeguard your mind, and you will begin to experience strength arise like you have never experienced before!

*My mind is servant to my will!*

# Take Action

Have you been a "rehearse the pain mama" or a
"meltdown mama?"

_____

_____

What are three steps to avoid negative thoughts?

_____

_____

_____

_____

What is the single action word to remember when dealing
with damaging thinking?

_____

This is my action step to create change in my thinking:

_____

_____

_____

_____

# Mother of Change

Life is filled with surprises, ups and downs, and valley seasons. The question is, "How will you respond?"

Will you be a meltdown mama, or will you rise up and choose to be a Mother of Change?

**Mother of Change defined:**

1. She is desperate for change within her family.
2. She is a chain-breaker!
3. She doesn't cower in the face of adversity.
4. She is victorious, rising above every circumstance.
5. She is a radical mom, meaning she uproots whatever doesn't glorify God in her home.
6. She is royalty.
7. She understands her place of authority within her home, established by God.

Mama, I believe the Lord has released a spiritual word to me for such a time as this! Yahweh wants his daughters to choose this day, whether they will be a diva mom or a warrior mom.

What is a diva?

A diva is defined as being self-important, temperamental, and difficult to please. She's materialistic and vain. She is immodest internally and many times, externally. She abuses her authority within her home for selfish purposes.

---

**The fear of the LORD is to hate evil;**
**Pride, and arrogance (Prov. 8:13)**

---

On the other hand, this is a warrior mom defined:

1.  She understands her personal value.
2.  She knows who she is and whose she is!
3.  She lives as a daughter of the Most High God.
4.  She is modest in heart.
5.  She is flexible and not temperamental because she understands that all things work together for her good according to scripture.
6.  She is not lackadaisical concerning her parenting responsibilities.
7.  She takes her mandate seriously to raise kids who will be the salt and light of the earth. She is willing to battle for them daily!

I believe the Lord gave me this illustration to define two moms that are direct opposites of each other.

In God's economy there is no such thing as neutral. He wants you hot or cold because if you are lukewarm He will spit you out! So,

I believe the Lord wants you to choose today. Will you be a diva or a warrior mom?

_____ Date _____

# *Prayer*

Father, thank You for giving me the mandate to raise children who will be the salt and light of the earth. Thank You that You will equip me to battle for them daily. Lord, open my eyes, ears, and heart to areas I can improve upon in our family. Help me to magnify Your ways in my household. Help me identify broken patterns in my life and show me how I have slipped from my guard duty. I'm ready, Lord. I am ready to be a soldier armed for battle. I am ready to be all-in. I am ready to be a Warrior Mother who is not easily moved. I am ready to be a Mother of Change. *I ask that You grant me the grace I need to walk with my eyes toward heaven and my heart toward change*. Help my family to live in one accord. Forgive me for wandering or becoming lazy in my spiritual walk at any level. Empower my family to stand united in fearing you with holy reverence. Keep us on the straight-and-narrow road, protect us, and guide us. In Yeshua's/Jesus's name, amen.

# Take Action

A Mother of Change is:

_____

_____

_____

_____

_____

A Diva Mom is:

_____

_____

_____

A Warrior Mom is:

_____

_____

_____

_____

What have you been living as?

_____

How can you change?

_____

A Mother of Change is a

Chain Breaker &

a Change Maker

-EmmaSara

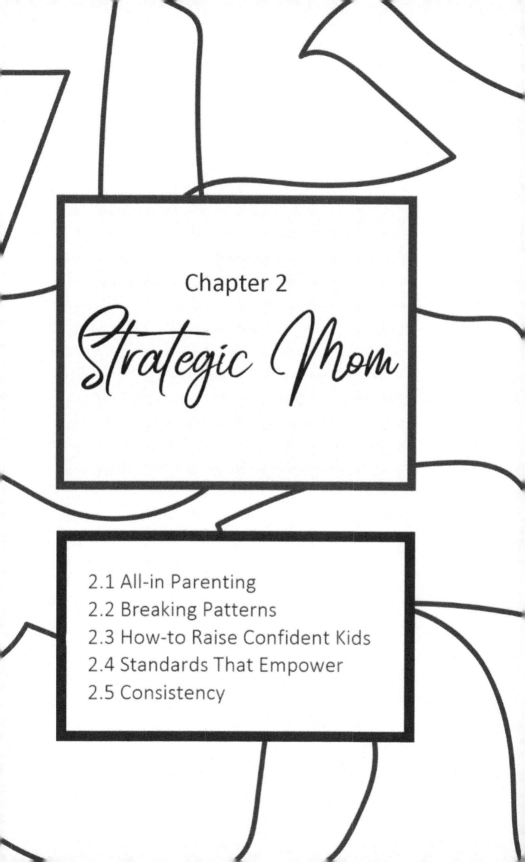

Chapter 2

# Strategic Mom

# All-in Parenting

Hey, Mama, have you experienced days that leave you feeling exhausted and like your last nerve is frayed? Sometimes you may feel like throwing up your hands and saying, "What's the point? These kids just don't listen!" Trust me, I understand. I wish I could say that my kids were angels all the time and obey immediately one hundred percent, but that would be a lie. So I can empathize with your frustrations.

In parenting, it common to wait until kids are older to try to step up parenting, but that's an invitation for sabotage! It's much easier in the long run if you put the energy in while they are young because once they become teenagers, you will receive the fruit of their early training. I know sometimes that is easier said than done. Believe me, I understand the frustration, despair, agitation, fatigue, and, yes, sometimes even anger that comes with parenting.

However, even with all the challenges of motherhood, I still consider myself an all-in parent. What defines the all-in parenting style? It's parenting that doesn't give up or give in no matter how daunting family life can get. There is also a strong focus on creating boundaries + order + structure with the family home.

This means that even if a parent is failing in patience and their kids are testing them, they remain consistent in keeping their kids accountable for their actions. So, it can also be considered a consistent parenting style.

To make it easy, remember this:

*An all-in parent =*

*A consistent parent*

I know you get tired, mama. I know you can get worn down, but don't give in, and don't give up! Stay the course and resolve to keep boundaries, order, and structure in your home. So many times, moms are tempted to be inconsistent in the early years of parenting because they figure their kids are small and too young to understand structure fully. Mama, I am here to tell you they can understand, and they can rise to the level of your standard. If you need help creating standards, we will cover that in this book too. So hold tight!

If you are experiencing current struggles in your home because you haven't been consistent, and this speaks to you, have grace for yourself, repent to God and your kids, forgive yourself, and stay the course. It may take more work because you started a little late, but better late than never. Especially now that you are learning about the Mother of Change mandate on your life, keep hoping, believing, praying, and decreeing. And most importantly, remain consistent in keeping your kids accountable for respecting and honoring you.

Are you ready to be equipped to be all-in?

In the following chapters, you will gain insight and wisdom to step into your power role. You will also learn about practicing consistency in different parenting situations.

I believe you can keep your parental focus. I believe you can rise to the challenge of raising world changers with confidence and fervor! Below is a prayer that can propel you in your decision to not only be all-in but stay all-in.

**Please note**: *Yahweh* is the Hebrew name for God, and *Yeshua* is the Hebrew name for Jesus. I am really into Hebrew root words, so it's my preference to use the cultural pronunciation for both.

# Prayer

*Yahweh, I thank you that you have called me to be a godly parent in season and out of season. Empower me to rise to the daily call with excitement. Prepare my heart and mind to stay consistent in training up my kids. I want to be a godly example of how they should live their life. Please, prepare my children to respect my godly counsel. Shine your light and love on us as we pursue living a family life that glorifies you. In Yeshua's name, amen.*

# Take Action

All-in parenting focuses on creating these three things:

_____

_____

_____

Short definition of all-in parenting.

_____

_____

_____

My confession and repentance:

_____

_____

_____

_____

_____

_____

My affirmation:

_____

# Breaking Unhealthy

## Patterns

This past April, I attended a personal development conference hosted by Eric Thomas, a world-class motivational speaker. During the event, ET spoke about the haves and the have-nots. The haves were noted as being in the 1 percent, those who have achieved great wealth and success.

I noted that he shared his story with a formula to shift his mindset. Afterall our mindset is where much of the battle is to break destructive patterns in our life.

*If you can change your thinking, you can change your life.*

There was a sequence in his message:

Observation + Lesson + Evidence + Personal Story/Problem= A Solution

**Observation:** He described to us how those living in the 1 percent of society had a certain lifestyle and mindset patterns for success.

**Lesson:** As a matter of fact, he experienced the most significant momentum in his life after he learned the specific lifestyle and mindset patterns of this certain group of people.

**Evidence:** To give us an *example* of how understanding patterns can usher in a quicker learning experience, he shared a story with us.

**Story/Problem:** He was having a hard time learning Spanish until he started to note the different patterns in the language. When he identified the unique patterns, things started to click and change for him in learning Spanish.

As I sat like a sponge to soak it all in, it left me thinking, if 1 percent of society has a similar lifestyle pattern, then the majority must have a separate lifestyle pattern as well. Eric's conference focused on teaching us about the habits of the 1 percent, but when I got home, I turned my **observation** to the habits of the 99 percent. At the conference, I noted the keyword was "patterns." There are patterns for success, so that means there must be patterns for those in lack, right?

After thinking it over and praying, I realized that there is **evidence** that many churchgoers have an over-emphasis on trying to break family curses and rebuking satan. In other words, there is a lot of praying going on, but change is not happening. Why? Why is this so?

The **story** is that many people put a big focus solely on binding and rebuking spirits when things become challenging or if they want things to change, which is 100% spiritual. Yet, they neglect the physical and tangible patterns—*generational bad habits.* I am not saying there isn't a place for such practices as binding and loosing. By all means, plead the blood of Jesus over your stubborn situations and break off generational spiritual attachments.

Just remember the **solution** is to do the spiritual work and follow it up with a tangible death to self. Deny your flesh. Deny your old habits. Say no to the old way of doing things. The spiritual groundwork doesn't have to keep getting repeated. Once it's done, it's done. The foundation is laid, and you can walk in total freedom: mind, body, and spirit.

If your history reveals a lot of drama even after you have repented, prayed, and rebuked the enemy. It probably has nothing to do with unbroken curses. Instead, the drama is probably lingering because your destructive lifestyle patterns haven't been willfully and mindfully changed yet.

*Stop repeating poor habits and reactions!*

It's time to wake up to your daily lifestyle patterns.

**Take a self-inventory of your reactions:**

1.  Outburst.
2.  Stinking thinking.
3.  Anger management.
4.  Jealousy.
5.  Depression.
6.  Eating for comfort.
7.  Stuffing emotions.
8.  Shutting down.
9.  Angry outbursts.
10. Bitterness or whatever unhealthy pattern needs to be removed from your life.

After you identify any areas that need to be irradicated, create new habits to help you defeat the old ones. Here are a couple of things you can do:

• Keep a journal and list areas that come up and find scriptures to help you break free for good.
• Line up scriptures and affirmations to give you extra encouragement for daily living.

Earlier I mentioned I went to an Eric Thomas conference; I strongly believe going to personal development conferences and taking self-improvement courses are worth their weight in gold. Keep that in mind because I will be releasing online courses throughout the year to empower you on your journey to build stability in your home.

When you break destructive patterns in your life, you will begin to identify chains breaking off your life and your children's lives! Listen! I hear the chains falling!

# Prayer

If you are ready, with your hands lifted high, repeat these words:

Yahweh, I am ready to break off negative family patterns in my life! I will not blame satan any longer for things I need to take personal accountability for! I thank you, Father, that by your work on the cross, I have everything I need within me to conquer bad habits in my life that cause nothing but friction. I repent for giving up ground to the enemy, because I have authority by your name, Yeshua, to stand against him. He is a defeated foe! I repent of succumbing to stinking thinking, a poverty mindset and allowing myself to be blinded to areas that need change. Father, open my ears and eyes to blind spots in my life. Help me live out my best life to glorify you. In Yeshua's name, amen.

Now, boldly proclaim I am a CHAIN-BREAKER.

Repeat it again!

**I am a CHAIN-BREAKER!**

One last time! **I am a CHAIN-BREAKER!**

Can you feel the resolve rising within you? When you are done with this book, it will no longer be business as usual! After you wake up and your feet hit the floor, the enemy will tremble because a Mother of Change is awake! Yes, *the greatest imprint you'll leave on this earth is to raise world changers* because long after you made your exit your legacy will continue through the lives of your children and their children! Even if you are an entrepreneur, your most important work as a mother should be to build up a family that will turn the world upside down for God!

Remember, the Lord has called us to be the salt and light to society. The best way we can add a salty savor to it is by producing a taste of heaven on earth. Let us live like we are calling heaven down to earth by how we live our lives.

Therefore, it is written:

---

Thy kingdom come.
Thy will be done on earth, as it is in heaven. (Matt. 6:10).

---

As a Mother of Change, your mandate is one of the highest in the land! Believe it, take ownership of it, and walk in the power and authority that the Father has bestowed upon you to bring change!

# Take Action

Take self-inventory of your reactions and list some patterns that need to be broken in your life?

_____

_____

_____

_____

_____

_____

_____

Write, "I am a chain-breaker:"

_____

_____

What's the greatest imprint you will leave on this earth?

_____

_____

_____

_____

Don't react!

Instead, Respond.

# Setting Standards

I believe family standards are the strength and fortification of a home. Creating a lifestyle agreement within your family to uphold certain practices will help your household remain united in daily living. God is a God of order, and He delights in families that stand united in word and deed.

The reason why I didn't start your journey with this topic first is because if your home is upside down, it can create big problems if you immediately try to start setting up new standards without dealing with any heart issues first. A mama must deal with personal heart issues first to make sure she is committed to upholding the standards set. Kids must see that you are serious when it comes to setting standards if you would like them to uphold them for generations to come. Yes, set standards you would love for your kids to uphold when they have your future grandchildren.

This topic brings to mind the Bible story of the Rechabites. The story of this family is told in the book of  . In short, it's about a man who made a decree for his family to follow. Generations after his death it was still respected and honored. The story is amazing to me. As you read on, keep in mind that their family standards were based upon conviction rather than particular scripture laws. This means

Yahweh did not command this family to abstain from alcohol or not to live in built houses. The instruction was based upon personal persuasion that was passed on from generation to generation, and the Lord delighted in their loyalty to their forefather!

Let's take a quick look at the story...

---

*It is recorded that the prophet took some Rechabites into the Temple and offered them wine to drink, and that they declined on the ground that Jehonadab, son of Rechab, their ancestor, had commanded them not to drink wine or other strong drink, or to live in houses, or to sow seed, or to plant vineyards, and had enjoined them to dwell in tents all their days. (Jewish Encyclopedia 1906)*

*The Rechabites, hungry and thirsty, refused wine when it was set before them, because of the command of their ancestor Jonadab. (International Standard Bible Encyclopedia)*

---

Basically, Jeremiah was prompted by the Spirit of Yahweh to go the Rechabite family and invite them into the house of the Lord and offer them wine to drink. The family declined the offer based upon their fidelity to their forefather's instruction. You can read about the story in Jeremiah 35:8-10.

Keep in mind that the period of their lifestyle of abstinence was two hundred plus years from the time the decree was originally made. This means for hundreds of years this family stuck to the standard set by their forefather!

God was so moved by Jonadab's descendants that He used their faithfulness as an object lesson to the house of Israel who couldn't keep faithful to Him for a single generation! Time and time again the children of Israel disobeyed Yahweh's laws and commands, and here was a group of people that remained faithful to heed the commands of their ancestors for generations even in the house of the Lord!

Now back to the story...

---

*Then came the word of the Lord to Jeremiah, saying ....*
*I sent to you all My servants the prophets, rising up early and sending them, saying, 'Turn now everyone from his evil way, amend your doings, and do not go after other gods to serve them; then you will dwell in the land which I have given you and your fathers.' But* **you have not** *inclined your ear, nor* **obeyed Me.** *Surely the sons of Jonadab the* **son of Rechab** *have* **performed the commandment of their Father,** *which he commanded them, but this people has not obeyed Me." (Jer. 35:13-16)*

---

It appears to me that Yahweh bestowed great blessings upon the Rechabites for their faithfulness to the standard set before them.

*And Jeremiah said to the house of the Rechabites, "Thus says the Lord of hosts, the God of Israel: **'Because you have obeyed the commandment of Jonadab your father,** and kept all his precepts and done according to all that he commanded you, therefore thus says the Lord of hosts, the God of Israel: "Jonadab the son of Rechab **shall not lack a man to stand before Me** forever."' (Jer. 35:18-19)*

It appears that God blesses those who make and keep standards that are created for the good of the family, so let's look at some more benefits of setting clear family standards.

When your child clearly understands what is expected of him or her, they will be left with daily choices to make. They can either choose to obey or disobey. Giving your kids a standard to keep, helps to clarify his or her character. It is much easier to see when kids are generating rebellion in their hearts when there are specific guidelines set out for them. When you know what you are dealing with, you can help a kid course-correct easier because you can go straight for the root, which produces the fruit. Picture a running track. It's much easier to run a track without hurdles than to have things to jump over. A life that is chaotic and without order creates hurdles. A lifestyle that has clear standards and structure provides a clear running track for your whole household to reach the finish line of each day. But when you are double-minded and constantly shifting the standard because you become worn out and tired or whatever reason, you end up creating hurdles for them. Did you hear that? Being a double-minded parent places hurdles in your family's life! It can hinder righteous living, which impacts who they become as adults. Remember, the goal is to raise children who will grow up to change the world.

World changers are decisive.

They are focused.

They have clear goals.

By setting standards that are clear and enforced, children learn the value of being single-minded. It's easier for anyone to obey when they fully understand what is expected of them. If you make a rule important one week and then make it of little significance the next, it can reinforce a satanic mindset. There is a heavenly mindset, and there is a satanic mindset. Anything that is counter to the Word of God is a satanic mindset and can cause double-mindedness.

---

*A double-minded man is unstable in all his ways. (James 1:8)*

---

Are your kids questioning their faith?

Are they questioning the Word of God?

Are they disobedient and rebellious?

**If so, consider your current home standards.**

1. Ask yourself if they line up with Biblical living.
2. More importantly, how are you doing in enforcing them?

3.  Are you personally living them out?

Your answers should provide some insight for you.

If you need help with developing more precise focus and goal setting, check out my book that I mentioned earlier, Passion. Purpose. Time Management.

Mama, pray with your family for God's direction in this area, then set your family standards and line them up with the Bible.

Some areas that you can set up standards for are:

1.  Friend groups
2.  Music
3.  Language
4.  Clothing
5.  Alcohol consumption

This list is just some areas to use as a jumping point.

Every family will have their own convictions; for example, our family chooses to abstain from drinking alcohol. I understand that people will say it is legal to drink in the Bible. However, I am no fool; I know any man can fall!

If a righteous man, like Noah, had a drunk family crisis, who am I to think that my children are not capable, especially when alcoholism runs in my family? So, I have personally decided to caution my kids against drinking alcohol; otherwise, they risk becoming alcoholics. I remind them that it doesn't matter if people say it is biblically legal because our family history shows a lineage of alcohol abuse.

So, I choose to abstain for the sake of my future generations.

Getting back to setting standards, be clear, concise, and led by godly conviction when you are ready to discuss your final decisions with your kids. Also, pray for complete and total unity in your entire household and that they would stand with you.

If you have been living without set standards, you may see some bucking. If you get resistance, stay focused on the goal of reaching their heart and press into Yahweh for His empowerment and wisdom. Every situation is unique, and Yahweh has your solution. Allow Him to do a work in your household. If you need more encouragement, see the Mom's Q & A section in the Appendix area in the back of the book.

---

*And the Lord said unto Jehu, Because thou hast done well in **executing** that which is **right** in mine eyes, and hast done unto the house of Ahab according to all that was in mine heart, thy **children of the fourth generation** shall sit on the throne of Israel. (2 Kings 10:30)*

---

# Take Action

These are two reasons setting standards are important:

_____

_____

_____

_____

_____

_____

Ask the Lord what standards He wants you to work on and

list them:

_____

_____

_____

_____

_____

This is my new conviction about setting family standards:

_____

_____

# Consistency

Consistency is one of the most impacting virtues you can practice in day-to-day parenting. I have counseled many married couples over the years, and one of the greatest handicaps in marriage is inconsistency in child training. If you are married to someone who is double-minded or unstable, you probably agree. Dear mama, let me go a little deeper. Maybe you are the inconsistent one in the marriage, or maybe you and your husband are both guilty of inconsistency. This book is like a one-on-one boot camp, so strap up your boots and lace them up tightly because we are about to journey on some bumpy territory, but don't turn back now! The end is on the other side of the hill if you can just stick with me. Will you venture further? In life, we will have struggles, but those struggles can be magnified when our personal character is lacking. Over the years, I have noted that many parents don't stay consistent with their kids because they get worn down, and sometimes it is easier to give in rather than remain consistent. However, I am reminded of how even horses are constantly testing boundaries. Horses are extremely intelligent and known for their independent behavior. If smart horses will test the boundaries, how much more will your intelligent kids? It is often said that horses have a mind of their own! They are known for finding any breaks in their corral, which the following article highlights.

*We've all known at least one equine escape artist. The crafty pony that figures out the grass really is greener on the other side of the fence. The amorous gelding that would prefer to live with the mares. The way-too-smart mare that knows how to open gate latches and lead everyone on a merry romp. I remember watching to see how one particular mare was getting out of her field, only to see her kneel down and sneak under the electric fencing—she had learned that her winter blanket protected her from being shocked! (Equine Wellness Magazine)*

Horses can be crafty, and kids will push the boundaries any way they can. So, be resolved not to make it easy for them by being inconsistent.

On another note, haveyou ever considered that consistency is a virtue? Are you teaching your children to value it? How important is it to you to keep your kids accountable in the areas of truth-telling, emotional and mental stability, having a good work ethic, and being kind to others? How important are those topics to you?

# Consistency + Correction =
# Building stability

I set my focus on not deviating from base standards, which creates security within my home. Yes, my convictions have grown over the years with time and maturity, and I do my best to live them out. Raising my kids with stability is a huge goal for me because I understand what is at stake if I don't. Sure, there are plenty of areas I fail in daily. I make mistakes like anyone else. If I don't crucify my flesh daily, I can be impatient and easily irritated. I used to have a sign on my kitchen cabinet that said, "Happiness is something you decide ahead of time." Admittedly, I'm still working on plenty of areas to improve upon in my life. However, when it comes to the topic of consistency, I'm dedicated to executing.

However, it is important to note that there was a time when I took advantage of my kids being small, which led to some of my past "mom failures." However, I'm someone who wants to grow from my mistakes. Basically, I am not trying to paint a perfect picture of myself. Every person has strengths and weaknesses, and consistency is a personal strength of mine. If it has been a struggle for you thus far, make little decisions moment by moment to keep you on track. Don't stray from what you say. If you say you are going to do something, do it. If you set a boundary for your kids, hold them accountable when they cross it. If you tell the kids no, let your no be a no. Remember the horse article? That horse will try to escape if they find a breach or hole to squeeze through. If you put them back in the boundary without fixing the fence, as soon as you look away, they will go right back to that breach. Children do the same thing. If they see a point of weakness in your parenting because of instability, they will wear you down until you crack so they can do what they want.

But, don't give up, don't back down, and don't give in!

---

*And let us not grow weary while doing good, for in due season we shall reap if we do not lose heart. (Gal. 6:9)*

---

Did you notice the verse above states, if you don't lose heart, then you shall reap? You will reap good things; good fruit, so keep up the work. Remain resilient to teach your child boundaries by rejecting their manipulation. When you set these practices in motion in your home, you will undoubtedly experience a change in your family life. If you become a more consistent mama, it will impact you as a wife, daughter, friend, and family member. It's true—when you decide to be more consistent, it may be met with resistance from anyone and everyone you deal with regularly. If they get upset, it's because they can no longer bend you. **This means you should embolden yourself not to be moved by tears, anger, frustration, or whatever manipulation is thrown your way.**

Remember, some people may not like that, so become comfortable with standing your ground.

When you do this, another character flaw, double-mindedness, will be simultaneously kicked to the curb because **inconsistency and double-mindedness** are two sides of the same coin. Now that is something to get excited about! As believers, we should desire to be stable: mind, body, and spirit. In the first chapter of James, it speaks of a double-minded man who is unstable in *all* of his ways. The verse doesn't say in *some* of his ways, but rather a double-minded man is unstable in *all* of his ways. Another look comes from the Greek word dípsyxos (pronounced dipsychos), which means divided interest. The root means to have two psychologies.

One study guide defines double-minded this way:

---

*A person "split in half," vacillating like a "spiritual schizophrenic.* (HELPS Word-studies)

---

A spiritual schizophrenic? It sounds severe and crazy, right? It is. What does double-mindedness behavior look like? It might be having a conviction and telling your kids no when they get an invite somewhere, but with a little whining and complaining, they influence your "no" into an "okay" or "whatever."

Another example could be setting a family standard and adhering to it for a week only to return to your old ways. It could mean that you are living as a "Sunday Christian." You know the type, party on Saturday and church on Sunday. As a parent, if you are double-minded, you become one of the household's weakest links. If your husband is double-minded, he is the weakest link. If both parents suffer from it, then look out! Sooner or later, you will inevitably experience some serious struggles, and your kid's faith will likely waver or be watered down. Of course, God can raise up a person from any kind of background to bring him or her to spiritual enlightenment and truth. However, that is the exception rather than the rule. So, don't gamble with being inconsistent and double-minded in your daily life. Let the thought of raising whole human beings be constantly on your mind. Set a standard of being steadfast with training them. Do it because it's right. Do it because you are a Mother of Change.

# Take Action

Fill in the blank. Then, write out your thoughts.

Inconsistency and _____ are the two sides of the same coin.

_____

_____

_____

One thing that really hit home for regarding the topic of consistency is:

_____

_____

_____

_____

_____

Three of my goals  for creating more consistency are:

_____

_____

_____

_____

*I will not be moved.*

— EmmaSara

# The Secret to Raising Confident Kids

What good mom doesn't desire to raise confident kids? Yet the lack of confidence in our youth is wavering just as much as it is for many moms. When I think of how much peer pressure kids go through, it makes me want to press in harder to help them solidify their personal identity.

---

*Society is so conflicted it seems, so many people want to stand out from the crowd, but they are doing everything they can to be clones of someone else.*

*What if everyone truly desired to be genuine and stopped trying to act like someone else? What would that look like?*

*The lure of tabloids and plastic surgery would diminish. The commercial industry would be in an uproar, no longer able to entice the masses. They would lose their power to seduce people into wanting perfection wrapped up in the latest and greatest brands.*

*Instead, people would understand that they don't "need" this or that to be a better or more attractive person. The world as we know it would turn upside down!*

*To read the rest of this chapter on personal identity, check out my book: **Passion. Purpose. Time Management.**- Finding your purpose. Fine-tuning your life.*

---

Unfortunately, as I was watching a program this week, I was reminded of how much children need to be freed from the pull of perfection defined by media. The series was on girls as young as eight years old sharing their physical insecurities. Little girls with gorgeous curls, glowing skin, and big eyes shared how they couldn't even look at themselves in the mirror because all they saw were imperfections. They shared all the popular terms used to describe body perfection and how they didn't line up with those definitions. Skinny girls thought they were fat, and countless teens were going under the knife to carve out society's definition of beauty on their bodies. As a mother watching these young girls, it made me sad and angry at the same time. I was sad that these girls were being blinded to their personal worth. All I saw was beautiful young ladies that were being attacked by a real enemy.

I was mad because they lost their self-confidence as they were bombarded with cultural lies. I need to say this; satan is on the warpath to destroy Yahweh's creation. He hates humanity. He hates that each of us where created in the image of God. So he is seeking to distort humanity via self-mutilation. This reminds me of an interview I saw on a popular show. It was about a young lady who got addicted to plastic surgery in her early twenties. She said she was miserable with herself. She hated her addiction, yet she told her surgeon she would get work done every minute if she could.

Remember, if satan can get people to hate themselves, he can get them to question God. If people start believing that Yahweh makes mistakes, this creates a domino effect allowing satanic influence into our lives. What does this look like played out? It looks like beautiful little girls viewing themselves as freaks of nature and seduce teenagers who are not fully developed to risk going into surgery to change what God has created. Worst of all, the most destructive outcome is suicide. Child suicide is escalating because satan is into destroying personal worth. Too many young people are giving into that lie.

Just a couple of hours ago, I watched a mom do a live video online because her handsome, loving teenage son committed suicide. Days before his death, he told his mom he saw the world for what it was. He was dealing with anxiety and depression, and he came to a point in life where he felt his life no longer had value, so he ended it. He lost confidence in humanity, and he lost confidence in himself. My heart was broken for this mom.

This got me thinking about a recent story I read about a baby that was found in a dumpster left for dead. He was rescued and adopted. He grew up to own a company that is worth millions. He shared his story about how he had to establish a strong self-confidence because kids were mean to him and called him the "dumpster baby." As I listened, I thought about how cruel kids can be. I was reminded that the enemy wants our kids to be defeated and lost. I was reminded that he will even use other kids to execute his plan to rob confidence. He wants our sons and our daughters. You will hear me repeatedly mention that I chose to homeschool my kids to protect and all these factors are the reason why. As I research today's youth, I see kids who are insecure, filled with anxiety and they are more confused than ever.

---

*According to the National Institutes of Health, nearly 1 in 3 of all adolescents ages 13 to 18 will experience an anxiety disorder. These numbers have been rising steadily; between 2007 and 2012, anxiety disorders in children and teens went up 20%.*

*What's causing the rise in teenagers with severe anxiety? How did we get here?*

*1. High expectations and pressure to succeed.*
*2. A world that feels scary and threatening 3. Social media (healthychildren.org- Anxiety in Teens Rising)*

---

I acknowledge that my kids could have easily fallen into those stats had they attended school. They would have fallen into peer pressure, and they would have self-confidence issues. How do I know this? Because even though they stay home for their education, satan has still been after my kids, and I have had to battle hard for them! Even with all the pouring into them that I do, the enemy has come and tried to lie to them about their worth. He's had momentary success, but I have been near them ready to battle fiercely. And, together with the strength of Yahweh, we have been victorious. This chapter focuses on sharing essential strategies with you because this topic should always be on the top of your priority list when you are praying for your kids.

Like I said, my kids have been raised to recognize their value, yet they still have their moments of self-doubt and insecurity. So how can we raise kids that will know how to snap back and not believe lies the enemy plants in their head about their value? Being that satan is a spirit being and the father of lies, I believe that we should war in the spirit! Stand on your authority in Christ to verbally tell the enemy to take a hike! Fast and pray for breakthrough for your kid. Why? Because much of our battle is spiritual with a physical manifestation.

---

*For we do not wrestle against flesh and blood, but against principalities, against powers, against the rulers of the darkness of this age, against spiritual hosts of wickedness in the heavenly places. (Eph. 6:12)*

---

The reality is that at some point in life, we will all experience a lack of self-worth to some degree. Of course, some will have an issue with it more than others. If your family wrestles with this topic on a grand scale, then make it a family goal to crush this area with the help of Yahweh! Kids are smart, and they are watching and listening! Mirror how you would like them to respond. When the enemy sends an attack on the mind, be an example of a proper response.

Are you ready to help your child become strong and unshakable when the storms of self-doubt try to come rushing in?

## 5 Steps to Build Confidence in Your Kids:

1. Mirror godly confidence.

2. Teach them how to identify when the enemy is attacking.

3. Teach them how to respond to the lies of the enemy.

4. Support a healthy mindset about personal value.

### Step 1 – MIRROR GOD CONFIDENCE

If you're someone who deals with a lot of self-rejection, you need to ask, not just pray, but ask God in Jesus's name to reveal where your lack of self-love is rooted. Once the area is revealed, renounce it. Tell it goodbye for good! Release your offenders to God, trusting He will practice justice on your behalf. If the spirit reveals acts that you have committed that have ushered in this unloving spirit, repent and thank God for His faithfulness and mercies that are new every day! If you are not happy with yourself and feeling stuck, it's probably because you don't fully understand your value or power in the kingdom of God, and I get that. Regrettably, it's not always taught in church, and it's not taught in as many homes as it should be. So, believing in your own personal worth first is imperative to helping your child take ownership of their identity. After you take steps to reconcile with yourself and others, then you can lead your children more effectively in this area. If you don't lack God-confidence, than praise the Lord! Use this step to look for ways to show more than telling. Kids will pick up on your lifestyle more than they will listen to your words. So show them what living with this confidence looks like in action. I mention this because my husband practiced his faith inwardly for many years. He wasn't really open with his prayer life, and many times I even wondered if he prayed for me. You can talk to your kids about your relationship with God, but please show them what it looks like in action.

- Show them how to handle adversity by boldly standing in your authority in Christ.
- Praying about everything and anything out loud where they can hear and see me. I also include them in praying with me.
- Show them that you are happy with who God made you, which is so important.

**Step 2 - Teach your children how to identify when the enemy is attacking.**

A lot of kids will live their life in auto-drive, just going about their day-to-day business without seeing the big picture. They go about life, feeling, and reacting. They feel emotions, and they do things like get up and go to school or get on social media with a total disconnect from the spiritual connection in their day. So, the enemy comes in and feeds them propaganda that they assume is their own thinking because "Why would it be popping up in my mind otherwise?" This can cause confusion and shame at so many different levels! It's no wonder society's kids are so lost! It's bad enough there is an influx of hormones that can cause emotional instability. Then add to that the endless smut marketing and media directed at them by the prince of this world, and you have a battle on your hands!

However, this will not be so for your kids! Your eyes have been opened, and now it's time to take back territory that the enemy has stolen. Even an inch is too much ground to give away! You can recover what has been encroached upon by teaching your child how to identify when the enemy is at work: enticing, lying, and luring. Warrior Queen, your duty is to take note when the enemy is at work in your child. Capture the moment and deal with the spirit before you deal with the child. This means asking the Lord to give you a discerning spirit concerning the spirit that is operating in your child. If you need more help in this area, join our online community for videos and discussion. See appendix.

After you discern which spirit is operating, help your child recognize that they have the power and authority to reject the spirit that is influencing them to do things that are contrary to scripture.

As a parent, it's so important to leave emotions on the back seat when dealing with your kids during these types of conversations. Remember to respond rather than react. I reserve my anger for satan and his workers of iniquity. I have made it my aim to create a safe place for my kids to come to me with any issues they are dealing with. It's important that they feel safe to be honest with me so I can help them get to the root of their misery or bad behavior. This takes some self-restraint for sure! Plenty of times I want to react rather than respond, but responding in the spirit to a spirit is always the most powerful choice. Many days much of my time is spent having an open dialog with my kids, together or individually, about how every decision they make in their daily life will directly impact who they become in the future. This helps them have a far-reaching focus that will position them for adulthood.

## Step 3 - Teach them how to respond to the lies of the enemy.

After your child can identify the work of the enemy in their life, they need to be taught how to have victory. Just recently, one of my kids (Called "Z" to protect their privacy) was being attacked with bad dreams, temptations, and self-rejection. The Spirit revealed to me that the spirit of death and destruction was visiting my home while I was out of town. I didn't panic or get distressed; instead, I got quiet before the Lord. I waited for strategy, and I prayed. Then, I asked "Z" to get alone with God in prayer. Afterward, "Z" opened up about what was going on and started off by saying, "I am bad. I am bad." I was quick to say, "No, you are not bad! You're a child of God, and you are experiencing a spiritual attack, and that doesn't make you bad. You are a young person that is experiencing some typical things for a kid your age, mixed with spiritual influence, but you can rise above this all!" Then very calmly but powerfully with full authority, I spoke to the vexing spirits and told them to leave in the name of Yeshua. I then had "Z" command them to leave. I looked at "Z" straight in the eyes and said, "You are a child of God with a powerful call, so the enemy is pressing, but he will not prevail!" I saw a total countenance change before my eyes, and the chains broke right off! Teaching kids to separate themselves from the demonic influences they are experiencing is so essential for them to have victory over poor choices. It goes back to teaching them that even though they may have failed, it does not make them a failure! Remind your child of this often and watch the relief wash over them when they make a mistake.

## Step 4 – Be a life coach.

In life, we will all have struggles and failures. This is the time you can be not only a cheerleader for your child but a life coach. My thirteen-year-old son has been studying for months to take a very technical certification course. He has passed all the practice tests with flying colors, but he failed two certification tests. He was broken because he studied hard, and each test costs $150 to take. He felt down about flunking and spending the money. I could have acted disappointed about the results and the cash, but instead, I chose to be his coach. I was right there to remind him that Benjamin Franklin had thousands of failed attempts before he got noted for his accomplishments. I took the time to open up a post about the life of Mr. Franklin and I read the story out loud to him. I could see relief flood over him as I asked him, "How many times have you failed that test?" He smiled and said two. The answer spoke for itself. Things were really not so bad. The test he is taking is for an Artificial Intelligence Certification that can lead to a six-figure salary in his first year in business. He would be one of the youngest to get the certification and he has already passed the practice tests. If you ask me there is a ton to celebrate. Getting our children to switch focus by providing a new mindset is a gift that keeps on giving. A great way to be exposed to new thinking is to listen to motivational videos together. Our family loves to listen and watch motivational videos while we do our housework. Eric Thomas is our personal favorite. Some others on our list are Lisa Nichols and my sixteen year old enjoys Maya Angelou.

---

*When a reporter asked, "How did it feel to fail 1,000 times?" Edison replied, "I didn't fail 1,000 times. The* lightbulb *was an invention with 1,000 steps." (Healthy-inspiration.com)*

---

Teach your kid how to create a life narrative that is focused on purpose. Help them develop a "why" for everything that they do. When a kid can focus beyond limitations of age and socioeconomic status without addictions to social media and teen drama, they are unstoppable!

*When a kid can focus beyond limitations of age, they are unstoppable!*

## Step 5 - Support a healthy mindset about personal value.

The world has a definition of worth that is based upon temporal things, social media likes, appearances, and materialism. It's crucial that you help your kids establish a personal value statement about who they are and who they desire to become. I am not talking about their occupation. I am talking about character and virtue. I ask my little boys all the time, "What kind of man do you want to be? Do you want to be responsible? Do you want to be a hard worker? Do you want to lead your future children in the Lord?" It's so important to help them focus on something more significant than their current self. They need to establish aspirations based upon who God is calling them to be, rather than allowing the world to set their target. In the Kingdom of God, the world's standard is of no value. By helping your children develop a clear conscious, and unwavering standard for themselves, you allow them to run the race of life with more clarity and precision.

On our podcast, my girls and I discuss the importance of kids understanding "who" they want to be, not just "what" they want to do for an occupation. Mama, you want it to be unnatural for your kid to be mindless about their future. My kids have shown an ability to contemplate their future as early as three years old! It's never too early to get them thinking about who they are becoming. And by the same token, it's never too late to find out.

Another way you can support a healthy mindset is by encouraging them to read the Bible each morning. For years now, all our kids know they need to read the Word before they do anything or read anything else. When they come to the breakfast table, they know I will ask what they learned that morning in scripture. I have taught them to look for something to obey or apply to their life each morning. With this practice, my kids have all become very knowledgeable about the Word. As a matter of fact, they know way more about chronological Bible history than I do. I find that kids have an innate ability to retain information that interests them. At least that is the case in our home. I wish I had the same retention!

In any case, it is essential to practice these four steps to build up your kid. By implementing them, you will be acting as a Mother of Change and Warrior Queen in your home. You will not only be ready to protect, but also to equip your children to stand against the enemy who comes to steal, kill, and destroy!

For more information on raising kids with a godly character, check out the Mother of Change Podcast on iTunes and Anchor.

# Take Action

These are 4-steps to help my child build confidence:

_____

_____

_____

_____

_____

This step needs the most focus right now:

_____

_____

_____

_____

Write out one accountability step you plan to take:

_____

_____

# Chapter 3
## Watchful Mom

# Be a Gatekeeper

Many parents want to believe the best in people, so they are too trusting, but naivety is satan's playground. I have yet to meet a grown person who told me they were molested by a total stranger when they were a child. Unfortunately, stories of perpetrators are shared with me year after year. The list of offenders is long and not limited to: dads, grandfathers, uncles, aunts, cousins, siblings, neighbors, schoolmates, school bullies, teachers, coaches, youth pastors, priests, and friends of the family are some of those listed as abusers. With such a list, it brings me back to my resolve to be a spirit-filled gatekeeper of my home.

*The Lord delights when we protect our children by being aware of the schemes of the enemy.*

I am constantly reminded that we should be as wise as serpents and as gentle as doves. I would describe myself as having a heightened awareness of potential threats regarding children. I know this topic can feel uncomfortable to read about, especially if you are someone who wants to believe the best in people. However, it is too important not to include in this book. If people go to a military boot camp to learn to protect civilians, how much more should mothers be trained to protect their own children? Does this topic make you feel uneasy? If so, ask the Father to reveal to you why you feel uncomfortable. I think something that is so woeful is when there is a pattern of abuse in a family. The pattern is when a mother has been hurt as a child; then later, her kids are also violated by someone she trusts. If that is your situation, I don't wish to cast shame. You are here because it's time to break the chains in your family. As a former director for a women's and children's safe house and recovery center, I have counseled many women over the years, too many to count. Some people assume that women who were harmed in their youth would be super vigilant and on guard with their children. However, I noted that in the cases I had to manage, it was as if a switch was turned off to potential danger in the mind of moms that were violated. Clients would choose to trust people with their kids, and the pattern would continue.

Did you know that many people that molest kids are not pedophiles, which means they aren't inclined towards children? They target kids because they have a moment alone with a kid and the insatiable lust problem flares up, so they take care of momentarily fulfilling their appetite. This means they use children to relieve their urge. Many kids get molested because parents let their guard down by making them an easy target for lust buckets to fulfill the lust of the flesh! I am not saying that is the situation in every case. However, I personally have a stack of stories from friends and family members that do fit the bill.

Oh, how satan must revel in the corruption and loss of innocence.

But the Bible says...

---

*Take no part in the unfruitful works of darkness, but instead expose them. For it is shameful even to speak of the things that they do in secret. (Ephesians 5:11)*

---

Mama, if your child has been victimized by someone you trusted, please know that I am not writing to heap condemnation on you. The Lord knows your family has suffered enough turmoil brought on by the enemy. Instead, let the words I am writing soak in and do some serious soul searching and make a powerful choice to put an end to generational abuse. You are a Warrior Queen Mother and gatekeeper of your home! You possess everything you need to put a stop to current and future abuse! You have the power! Choose to be a chain-breaker and gatekeeper of your home.

---

*Look carefully then how you walk,*
*not as unwise but as wise,*
*making the best use of the time,*
*because the days are evil. Therefore do not be foolish, but understand what the will of the Lord is.*
*(Ephesians 5:15-17)*

---

Mamas everywhere should pray over their future grandchildren, that they would not be victims but victors in life!

As Warrior Moms, let's stand united to pray for each other in this area!

1. Let us band together to break generational victimization.

2. Let us stand united in protecting our children!

3. Let us agree for bondage breaking for all that read this book, and cry out to Abba for renewal and healing. We pray over the tears of remorse, for the aches of mistrust, and for the road to recovery to be swift.

4. Let us agree for total family restoration, for strength to flee from old patterns, and for a generational awakening, plus the empowerment for your future legacy! Amen.

If you think that none of this applies to you, let me tell you a short story. When I was in high school, I had a peer counseling class. Our teacher had our class grouped into counseling groups. Each group had ten students in it. We all grew very close during our semester together. As it turned out, eight of the ten students in my group were molested, and some only recently had gotten free from their perpetrators. Out of those that had been violated, 100 percent were perpetrated by someone their mom knew and trusted. I can clearly remember some of the specific violators sticking out in my mind: the teen neighbor, the stepdad, and even an aunt. Out of the eight students, only one of them reported to her mom about what was happening. She also shared with us how no one in her family believed her initially, which is why the other seven said they didn't tell. I was one of the two that didn't have such a traumatic experience.

However, I was victimized, even if it was just a first-stage offense. The fact is that I had a nine-year-old friend of the family who repeatedly tried to molest me when I was five years old. She cornered me on various occasions and tried to stick her tongue in my mouth, she attempted to show me pornography, and she got me under a sheet "house" one time to play "mommy and daddy." She grabbed me and stuck her tongue in my mouth and touched me on top of my clothes in areas that were off-limits to her! I ran away from her repeatedly. However, I never told my mom because I was only warned of men harming me, not other children, so I wasn't sure what to make of it. Unfortunately, like many children, I said nothing. Praise God I was not around her all the time because the handful of times I was she tried each time! The point is that you may think your child has never had a bad experience, but you could be wrong if you haven't developed a safe place for them to come to you with their cry for help.

I have one last story about this topic. I used to babysit a friend's niece that was around one year old. I was only nineteen, but I already had a heightened alert for kids who had been violated. As I was changing her diaper, I had this uneasy feeling that what I was seeing was not a diaper rash, but something more. In my spirit, I felt like she was being abused. I took my concern to the grandmother of the little girl, and she laughed at me like I was crazy and said it was absurd to think such a thing because they only leave her with people they trust, besides the fact that she couldn't believe anyone would harm a baby in such a way! I left very frustrated and even angry because she was so naive. I didn't babysit again after that. What she should have done was taken note of the baby's body condition, meaning to check her diaper area to look for changes when she was around other people. She could have taken the baby to the doctor as well for a checkup if something didn't seem right. Of course, it would be prudent to go to a family doctor that you have a good relationship with and trust. Try and be upfront with them. Just let them know you aren't sure about what you are seeing as in, "Is this normal for babies?"

In some cases, it may not be conclusive, but it's something to check off the list to try and figure out what's going on. The grandma could have also asked the brother, who was a few years older, some questions. He was extremely protective of the baby, and now I know why! There are many signs of sexual abuse, be educated on what to look for. (Please see the Appendix section for a comprehensive list)

About two years went by when I received a phone call from my friend. He was calling me to let me know I was right; his niece was being violated by a family member the whole time! A neighbor caught him! My stomach was in knots about it! That poor baby endured the first years of her life with such an atrocity because of naivety. I always say, "Ignorance is bliss, but at what cost?" Isn't it at the cost of innocence? Have you heard enough to become resolved to learn how to fortify your home even more? I hope so. Read on, because there are multiple gates a mom should protect.

## Prayer

Father, help me to walk as the wise and not the unwise. Help me to make the best use of my time. Show me how to protect my kids because I know the days are evil. Help me not to be foolish in raising my children. Help me to understand what Your will is, Lord.

In Yeshua's name, amen.

# Take Action

After reading about being a gatekeeper I am prompted to review the following area in my family's life:

_____

_____

_____

_____

_____

I am ready to repent of:

_____

_____

I am ready to be a better gatekeeper by:

_____

_____

_____

# The Eye Gate

We live in a time where there is a visual assault at every corner! Our kids are bombarded with unsavory images all over the internet and even when we go shopping! I'm at the point where I try to avoid taking my sons to certain malls because of seductive window ads. It is like a visual attack of the worst kind at every corner. The enemy would love to steal innocence from your small children and entice your older ones by putting images before their eyes that tempt and seduce a young mind. My question to you, mama, is this: Are you serving up perversion for your home? Or are you teaching your child how to guard their eye gate by setting standards that will instill godly values in them?

I know if a kid wants to really view smut, they can do it somehow. If they are breaking standards and going against safety rules, watch out because you have a real problem on your hands that must be dealt with quickly. The question is not whether kids are capable because I know they are. The question is whether or not you are allowing their eye gate to be seduced. It's time to learn how to identify the enemy lurking in your space. This is your territory I am talking about, your home. Let a holy fire rise from within you that acknowledges that you are the guardian of your children! Rise up and create a standard for your home! Set up your boundaries, and don't back down! Satan is a liar, and he would love to belittle nakedness because he knows that passivity in this area breeds perversion, heartache, and addiction! Understand the enemy wants your children to fall, and he is seeking to consume their souls because he is the author of family destruction!

Just remember, as Warrior Queens, we do not allow society to set our standards for righteousness. We set our standards-based upon scripture through prayer and/or our personal convictions. I rely heavily on godly convictions to protect the eye gate.

If you are a mama who depends on the Bible for life instructions, then do a word search on "nakedness" in scripture and let the Spirit lead you. We have studied the topic in-depth, and we have embraced God's word. We keep our eyes from nakedness. We don't expose our nakedness, and most importantly, we recognize that satan works to make nakedness "natural" and common because He opposes Yahweh and all of His commands. Still, they omit that Yahweh immediately clothed them post falling. He could have left them uncovered, but He did not. He then went on to instruct His children repeatedly that exposing nakedness is a sin. Have you ever noticed how much nudity is portrayed in art? It is a systematic breakdown of our senses. I am unashamed to state that I don't see nudity as a form of art. I believe open nakedness is opposed to scripture, which repeatedly instructs us to cover nakedness. Leviticus 18 is candid about nakedness.

Some Bible translations do a disservice by limiting the passages to avoiding sexual relations with family members. When I did a deep dive into the verses, I found a greater context. The interlinear translation gave a more authentic look at the verse. The Hebrew root word for *"uncover" is the word galah.* Galah can be broken down to mean: to discover, or show oneself, or revealed. *Nudity is ervah. In no specific order, some of the word descriptions are a shame, nakedness, indecency, and improper behavior.* So, keep these definitions in mind when studying this topic for a more precise understanding of Yahweh's standards for this topic.

One particular story that always sticks out in my mind is about the tabernacle in Exodus 20.

It gives instructions about omitting steps from the temple construction leading up to the altar.

---

*"Nor shall you go up by steps to My altar, that your nakedness (ervah) may not be exposed on it" (Exod. 20:26).*

---

To connect that principle to today's standard, that means men's gym locker rooms would have been out too, I am assuming.

Another illustration of the shame of nakedness is about Noah and his sons. It's important to note that the two initial falls of society include an acknowledgment of nudity. First with Adam and Eve and then again with Noah. This is not an old covenant/new covenant situation because it pre-dates Abraham or Israel.

Unfortunately, as the story goes, Noah got drunk. Yes, the same man that was considered righteous enough to be commissioned to build a lifesaving vessel for his people got wasted to the point that he was exposed, and it was considered a shame.

Basically, we have made it our focus as a family to adopt a mindset that your family may consider adopting too. As a family, you could agree with this statement:

*We don't do what we are allowed to do. We do what we are called to do!*

As you know, there are plenty of things considered "legal" in Christianity, even though they are not beneficial. However, we live according to wisdom and knowledge set forth by our convictions through prayer. I know there will be some that want to argue the scriptural details. However, I would respond by telling them if you're going to expose your kid to nakedness and expose their nakedness, you will have to deal with the potential consequences. Remember, satan wants you to expose your body and your children's body. He is like a lion seeking whom he can devour. He comes to kill, steal, and destroy. He looks to break down your senses so you can become naive. The best way he knows to destroy homes is through molestation and violation. Do not serve up your children or yourself for his purposes.

If you are still struggling with this area. Don't take my word for it. Press into God and ask the Holy Spirit to reveal what He wants you to learn about this topic. Jerimiah 33:3

reminds us that we can call on Yahweh, and He will show us great and unsearchable things we do not know. I share because I care, I don't get into scriptural debates on things I have a personal conviction about like protecting my kids from perversion. Even if I never read instructions about it in the Bible, I would still have my standard. I don't need a scripture to avoid alcohol, and I don't need one to avoid nakedness. I have grown children who have not been violated, and some have made it to adulthood without any addiction.

With today's stats, that is a big deal that I don't take lightly.

I will mention what my kids do once they are older and outside of my covering will be between them and the Lord, but let it be known I warred for them while they were under my care. I pray they stay the path that we have set before them. Maybe you are thinking your kids are not capable of doing such things like looking at inappropriate images or becoming an alcoholic. Beware, Mama! Don't be naive! I have witnessed signs of porn use by teen boys and talked to their mamas about it, and they were totally oblivious and in denial only to find out later how blind they were! Don't think your son is not capable.

Never be naive and think that your circle is above reproach, including your neighbors, friends, or your own children. The unfortunate truth is that kids get molested, and some are molested by other kids, plus some of them view inappropriate images together. This all happens because they are going under the radar. Let me tell you that both kids and adults are excellent liars when they are participating in sin.

Now check out these stats with prayer and seek God if your kids fall into these numbers.

*In a study of people ages 18–26, roughly two thirds (67%) of young men and one half (49%) of young women agree that viewing pornography is acceptable. In that same study, nearly 9 out of 10 (87%) young men and nearly one third (31%) of young women reported using pornography.*[24]

With those kinds of stats, you should feel a holy concern come over you about today's youth. Please, don't ever fall for the lie that porn is normal for boys or men to view! There is nothing okay about pornography!

*But I say to you that whoever looks at a woman to lust for her has already committed adultery with her in his heart. (Math 5:28)*

It may be common, but it should never be considered normal healthy behavior. Satan would say it's normal. God would say...

*Flee sexual immorality. Every sin that a man does is outside the body, but he who commits sexual immorality sins against his own body. Or do you not know that your body is the temple of the Holy Spirit who is in you, whom you have from God, and you are not your own? (1 Cor. 6:18)*

As providence would have it, Ephesians 5:3 popped up in my Bible app just before I came to write today, and there it was straight from the word, more confirmation.

*"But fornication and all uncleanness or covetousness let it not even be named among you, as is fitting for saints." (Eph. 5:3*

The translation for fornication is porneia. If you didn't catch on yet, porneia is the root word for pornography, and it should not be practiced or allowed within the body of believers or in our homes. I admit that when I was first married and living in Greece, I bought a statue that was topless along with other "art" pieces. Some friends who were mature in Christ tried to tell us of the dangers of bringing in these pagan statues into our home. But we thought they were just religious, and we ignored their caution until the Lord dealt with us and personally grabbed hold of us. When our eyes were opened, my husband took them outside and crushed them to powder, and we repented heavily for our rebellion. Not only was it nakedness, but it was also pagan idols! What were we thinking!

Mama, don't let your guard down. I can't say that enough: be on guard! Stand fiercely at your post, Warrior Queen!

I understand that at any point, our kids can turn from godly righteous living to corruption, and if they do, beware! Crank up your attention and prayer life for them immediately and continuously. Personally, my husband and I do our best to have as many safeguards as possible set-up for our kids, and even still, I am not saying concerning behavior can't or won't happen. Like many other families, we have had our moments with some of them dealing with temptations, but we battled hard, fasted, and focused on building trust and strengthening our relationship. Each time we have come out victorious and in good standing with our kids, praise God.

My goal as a Warrior Queen and a Mother of Change is to make it as hard as possible for the enemy to entice my children away. Our family tries to identify open portals around the house, and we stay vigilant to have checks and balances in place. For our boys, that means we have a code word when we are out. If we see a woman walking our way with all of her "business" hanging out, we call out our code word, and the boys know to look at their shoes until the temptation passes. We also have protection software on all the kid's computers, and none of the boys can be online in their rooms. If my sons are online, they must be in the living room with their screen facing everyone. We also have a phone standard. We decided our sons can't have a cell that has internet search access. So, my oldest son, who is eighteen, has a particular phone for firefighters. It's not a smartphone. Basically, we have decided that smartphones are not safe for our boys at any age. We are not willing to give up ground by giving into "portal phones."

"Portal phones" are gateways for satan to enter our home. They are too hard too monitor. We have all made a covenant with our eyes not to gaze upon improper images, watch inappropriate movies, or be comfortable with any immodesty. I think it's important to mention that even with all these safeguards and verbal commitments, some of them have admitted to certain temptations. They have expressed gratefulness for parameters to help them stay on track. I know the enemy is always lurking and just waiting for someone to let down their guard! Let us all remain watchful and teach our kids to be aware of the snare of the enemy.

Please pray about this topic and ask the Lord what areas you can become more vigilant in or what commitments you can make to live a more consecrated life.

# Take Action

Two areas I can be more vigilant in:

_____

_____

Two areas I will commit to pray for my child/ren:

_____

_____

Fill in the blanks: In a study of people ages 18–26, roughly ___ thirds ( _____%) of young men and one _____ ( _____%) of young women agree that viewing pornography is acceptable.

How do you feel about those statistics?

_____

Write out a personal prayer asking God to help you be

more sensitive to the areas of modesty and sexual

immorality:

_____

_____

_____

_____

# Ear Gate

Music has the ability to move the soul and lift the spirit. By the same measure, it can cultivate sensual feelings or send you into deep depression. I realize that music is not a big issue for some people. I know several people who think music is bleh and they aren't moved by it. If that describes you, please don't overlook protecting the ear gate for your children. It's important to guard our ears against unsavory music and dialogue just as much as it is to protect our eyes from viewing inappropriate images. I am going to share my personal journey with music with you because I think it's important to understand that music can be a lot more powerful than we think. Some music is destructive by the lyrics it contains, and music can also be worshipped, yes even Christian music. Sometimes the words are fine, but satan can still use all genres of music to open doors spiritually.

I will tell you this can be a hard topic to tackle for me because I was raised with music. My parents were teens when they had me, and music was a place where we had a common ground between us. We were pretty disconnected a lot of the time, but when the musi c came on, we would be dancing and smiling together. Music creates a happy place for me, and I know it can release endorphins in our body.

I can be a pretty serious grinder and not worry about having fun, but play some good tunes, and all that changes. With that said, I decided many years ago when my children were born to give up my secular music collection. I knew it was the right thing to do. Since I know the ear gate can be another way the enemy can enter our home and create a portal, I must focus on dying to the flesh as much as possible when it comes to music. Before I got my life right with Yahweh, I used to be a huge partier. I used to go to underground raves and dance until the early morning. The music was hypnotic, and I could stand right in front of the huge speakers and enter another universe, an evil one. It was like a drug for me. The music was always intoxicating by itself. In the most basic sense, I truly understand the power of music, and I understand that it's not always the content that makes something okay to listen to or not. Part of the reason I know I have to stay on guard in this area is because one night, I had a prophetic dream where the Lord showed me I was still worshipping music even if it was faith-based! Ugh! When I woke up, I clearly understood! The father was asking me to stop worshipping faith-based music.

Remember, there are wolves in sheep's clothing, even in the Christian music industry. In some cases, the lyrics can be completely kosher (scripturally sound) and still be problematic for a believer if the beat overrides a person's ability to pull back and survey a song. As I mentioned earlier, music can be seductive, hypnotic, rage producing, lust producing, and can conjure up the flesh easily. This is why we have to guard with what we personally listen to and what are children are listening to. All Christian music is not neutral. A very popular "Christian worship" group had to

126

remove a music video they had online because too many people started to feel suicidal tendencies after watching it. Mama, music that creates such feelings is not rooted in Christ. The group told on itself with that song. They are wolves in sheep's clothing. I believe there are many "Christian" bands that are commissioned by satan to seduce our kids. Satan wants to appear as harmless but be on guard! Some groups have a direct mission, and others are just in the industry for money with no spiritual purpose. Unfortunately, just as the church has many weeds that grow up alongside the good stalks of grain, so does the music industry. Some music artists enter the music industry through the Christian genre because it can be easier to get into than the secular industry. The intent isn't really about glorifying God with their music as much as it is about growing a following and an audience. This means there can be a spiritual confusion interlaced into music because of the artist who is creating it.

For people like me who have already had a problem with worshipping music, this can be problematic because the pull of the flesh is strong. If the artist begins with a flesh intent, it is easy to interweave the flesh element into music. As I write, I have to be honest with you. I didn't want to write about this since I honestly still need to keep it in check, and I know people can be so judgmental. Thankfully God is gracious with us because many people are not.

So let me share the rest of my music journey with you. For about five years, I did a music fast from certain genres of music. I did it because I felt a deep conviction to do so for not only myself but the kid's sake as well.

During that time we listened to a lot of classical music and hymns. It was a good season of learning to subdue our flesh. In the more recent years, we re-expanded our music selection because we are in the media business, and we create a lot of video content, and let's face it; music can make or break a production. We understand the power and sway of music, so we do add it to our productions. Just think of a major film and the soundtrack. What would it be without music? I am not trying to call out certain genres of music. I am not saying all music with a beat is bad. I am just saying I have had a personal issue worshipping music in the past. This is a topic I must be cautious with. I must set boundaries for myself and my kids. You might be asking yourself, "What does that look like?" Once upon a time that looked like complete abstinence from any beat-driven type of Christian music.

Now, I have taught my kids to view some music selections like a decadent sugar-filled dessert. We are a low-sugar-eating family, so we only eat sugary desserts once in a great while or for a special occasion. Music is the same way for us. Sugar is not completely off-limits, but we do limit it. I wouldn't eat chocolate brownies made with sugar every day, but I wouldn't have a problem eating an occasional piece. The best way I can describe our relationship with music is that my family has boundaries as we do with the food we eat. We understand that sugar is not something to be consumed often, and we understand "sugary" music is not beneficial for us daily either.

We understand music is an important element in video productions, so we use it with care. We use it with intentionality. We survey each song and come to an agreement on what we use. Basically, I am teaching my kids to take ownership of music, or it will own them. I have noted that my older kids will choose to fast certain music for short seasons. When they are battling with the flesh, they will shut down some selections, and I respect and support that move of death to self. I know when I must lay off fatty foods and stick to salads and lighter food only. It's no different with music. The key is to establish an inner voice of caution within yourself and teach your kids to do the same. Many times, kids are not taught to have a voice of caution concerning music, which can be dangerous.

I did a listening exercise with my girls last summer. I turned on a Christian music video and turned the screen away from them so they could only hear the words and music. The words seemed to be edifying from a scriptural observation, it wasn't a loud song, and it wasn't a bumpin' song. It was kind of quiet. I let them survey it because the video was alarming to me, and clearly there was a spirit of deception behind it even though it was from a popular Christian church worship band. They both listened without watching, and they both said, "NO, NO, it's not good. There is something dark about it." When I showed them the video, they were just as creeped out as I was. It is one thing for a secular song to have words that are not edifying spiritually, it's a no-brainer not to listen to it. It's easy to have no expectations for it. But when a song comes on that is supposed to be safe yet is shadowed with darkness, I think it's a whole different level of caution because it is done in a spirit of deception. This craftiness is what troubles me the most and leads me to be on guard.

At the end of the day, I think it's important to invite caution into our life when it comes to music. I believe it's important to ask the Spirit to give us personal boundaries when it comes to music. I am not interested in trying to be music police for anyone. Besides, who has time to worry about what others are listening to? I understand something might be fine for you; that's not okay with me or us and vice versa. My family may listen to things that you're not okay with, let each of us live our lives before God. Stay open to His guidance in this particular area because it's before Him and Him alone that we each stand or fall.

This section is not written to cast shame or judgment on anyone. Nor do I hope to invite any upon our family concerning the music we listen too. I hope that you will be piqued to petition God about this area and search your heart before Him concerning the topic of protecting the ear gate for yourself and children. Don't forget to pray that your kids will become sensitive to what the spirit is saying concerning this area. Our family uses personal reflection when it comes to music by asking ourselves some of the following questions to test what we listen to.

## Surveying Music

1. Is my spirit strong enough to listen to this right now?
2. Is my flesh trying to rule me this week?
3. Is this song causing me to slide back to past worldly habits?
4. Is this just a bite of an occasional brownie, or is this a gluttonous gorging and too much of a tasty thing?

I suggest taking time to pray and seek the Lord on this topic. When you get your answer, make sure to journal it.

## Prayer

Father, thank you that your mercies are new every day. Thank you for leading me in the way I should go, so I can lead my children in living a righteous life that pleases you. I am asking you to reeducate our family about music and worship. Give us an ear to discern and a heart to desire caution. Help our family to be in one accord on this matter. In your name, Yeshua, amen.

# Take Action

I should invite caution into my life regarding music because:

_____

_____

_____

_____

_____

List two questions to survey music:

_____

_____

_____

Pray about the music you are listening to or your children are listening to and list any thoughts that come to your mind when you are done:

_____

_____

_____

_____

*I am a Gatekeeper.*

# The Mouth Gate

Protecting the mouth gate shouldn't be overlooked because it's not what goes into the mouth that defiles, but what comes out. So, your family must recognize that there is power in words. They can bless or curse. This year I watched a video of an educational study done in a large school for the students to learn the impact of words. There were two large house plants placed side by side under glass. They had the same amount of light and water. However, there was a difference in what the plants heard underneath their glass through the speakers.

All-day long, one plant heard affirming words about how healthy and beautiful it was, while the other was told negative words about how ugly and terrible it was. Within a short amount of time, the results were clear that the plant that was spoken to with words of life flourished while the other one was beginning to wilt and on the verge of death! It was clear to everyone who viewed the changes that if this happened to plants, how much more could it happen to people?

Negativity begets negativity. It feels contagious sometimes, and we need to put a stop to it in our daily life for ourselves and our children. Instead, teach your kids how to use the power of words not only to bless others but also how to call-in provision for your family. The poverty spirit is alive and well in many homes because family members are always saying how broke they are and reciting how they have no money. I have made it a habit to say, "Money is not a problem, and I have more than enough to do what God has called me to do." Ever since I started this practice, the Lord has sent supernatural deposits. One month, we even received a $30,000 increase! Talk about a blessing. I believe God's word about having plans to prosper us and give us hope for our future. Claim that truth for yourself too, and your family. Our words are powerful, with a bad or good impact. I should mention that I have noticed that I can fall back into calling out my kids' bad habits, and then they will get worse! However, when I choose to lavish them with blessings, and I proclaim what I want them to be, they become it.

Here are some affirmations you can speak over your kids.

**My kids are:**

- Clean.
- Mindful.
- Respectful.
- God-fearing.
- Not given to temptation.

Mama, your tongue is powerful; with it, you can build up or tear down. What are you going to choose? I plan to revisit this chapter, often myself! I hope you will too.

# Take Action

My mouth has the power to:

_____

_____

The plant lesson showed me:

_____

_____

_____

Three affirmations I will say over my kid/s:

_____

_____

_____

_____

_____

_____

_____

_____

# Chapter 4

## Warfare Mom

# Stand Against Hypocrisy

"Do as I say, not as I do." How many times have you heard that statement in life? Did your parents ever tell you that growing up? How did that make you feel? When it comes to setting up character and virtue standards in your home, do you expect what you are not willing to give or do? Do you live as an example of what you desire your kids to practice in their daily life? Or are you making excuses for your behavior? Kids are more prone to copy what you do rather than what you say!

Does your kid have a problem with not accepting instruction? How do you respond to authority? Is your child having problems with jealousy? Do they catch you making faces when someone is succeeding? Do you wish your kids were calmer and not so erratic? Are you emotionally stable or given to mood outbursts?

Do your kids constantly blame other kids for their actions? How are you doing with taking personal accountability for yourself? The point is, self-check. Kids have a hard time respecting someone who is double-minded, and there are so many scriptures speaking against this character flaw that it puts a holy fear in me.

As these people draw near with their mouths and honor Me with their lips, but have removed their hearts far from Me.
*(Isa. 29:13)*
*I hate those who are double-minded, But I love Your law.* *(Ps. 110:113)*

Hypocrisy and double-mindedness walk hand and hand. You cannot have one without the other.

The Webster's 1828 dictionary gives the following definitions for each of these character flaws:

*Double-minded: Having different minds at different times; unsettled; wavering; unstable; undetermined*

*Hypocrisy: A concealment of one's real character or motives. More generally, hypocrisy is a simulation, or the assuming of a false appearance of virtue or religion; a deceitful show of a good character, in morals or religion; a counterfeiting of religion.*

In God's eyes, sin is sin, no matter how small. So we should assume that He desires us to be stable and consistent in our lives down to the smallest detail because scripture states, "a little leaven, leavens the whole lump." *In other words, just a small amount of double-mindedness impacts the WHOLE family!* Remember, in scripture, the Lord was the most severe with the Pharisees because they were hypocrites of society.

Let's do a little recap from an earlier chapter: Do you have a conviction that leads you to make a specific decision, but with enough pressure or complaining, you cave and give in? If so, you are double-minded. Do you set standards in your home only to allow kids to break them, or worse, you break them yourself? You are double-minded. Do you tell your kids that it is important to serve God but go on living daily life without any differences from the world when you are away from church? That is hypocrisy at work. Repent! Repent to Yahweh. Repent to your kids and stay true to your word. Be consistent with your lifestyle and stop making excuses for your hypocrisy. All you are doing is robbing yourself and your kids of a blessing. Being unstable with your decisions allows the enemy to get in and take up residence in your home!

Don't give up territory! You give up ground by wavering and being unstable in your daily walk.

If satan loves when you are unstable, then make a resolve not to be his puppet any longer! He cannot invade your space unless you allow him to by leaving your gate open! Fortify the entrance of your home by choosing to be stable in all your ways, and in doing so you will magnify God.

# Prayer:

Father, please reveal areas in my life where I need to repent. Lord, fortify my mind. Help me to be single-minded and only focused on doing your will. Strengthen me to be an example to my children of godly living without excuse. Continually guide me in all that I do so I may glorify you with my life, especially as a mom. In Yeshua's name, amen.

# Take Action

How much double-mindedness impacts the whole family?

_____

_____

_____

Give a personal definition of hypocrisy:

_____

_____

_____

List a scripture reference from this section that spoke to you:

_____

_____

_____

_____

Areas I need to repent for hypocrisy:

_____

_____

_____

I do as I say.

—Emma Sara

# Identifying the Victim Mindset

In life, falling is inevitable, but it's not about how we fall that has the greatest impact on our lives, but how we rise! Raising resilient human beings is always at the forefront of my mind, and it drives me as a mother. As a Warrior Mother, it is so important to focus on detecting when the *victim spirit* is operating in your home. In this case, we view this offender as both a *spirit and a mindset*. It's important not to belittle the fact that this mindset has a spiritual aspect to it as well. This understanding leads me to call out a victim spirit when I identify certain behaviors in my kids.

---

*For we wrestle not against flesh and blood, but against principalities, against powers, against the rulers of the darkness of this world, against spiritual wickedness in high places. (Eph. 6:12)*

---

While anyone can have this type of mindset, I find that people who suffer from it, consistently do so because of generational ties and influences, spiritual and otherwise. In our home, I have a zero-tolerance policy for tolerating it.

This spirit creates a black hole in the soul that can never be filled by any human. If you have a child that is super needy, no matter what you do, you may be dealing with a victim spirit that produces a victim mindset. They are two sides of the same coin.

Many parents feel guilty for not being able to meet their children's needs properly when they are acting out with this mindset. However, I am here to tell you to stop feeling guilty. Stop feeling inadequate if you are truly trying your best. This paradigm of thinking doesn't only reside with kids, but also with adults. So, it's critical to identify negative behaviors and deal with them on the spot. They must be dealt with as soon as they appear. It takes a lot of energy to deal with this behavior. However, if you are consistent and persistent and remain in prayer over it, you will see good fruit. Mama, become educated in identifying the signs of this consuming spirit operating in your home!

## 10 Signs of a Victim Spirit/Mindset:

1. Lack of accountability for personal wrongdoings.

2. Always breaking things yet says, "It's an accident."

3. Lying and crying when you call them on things.

4. Emotionally unstable and cries as a first response when faced with any uncomfortable situation.

5. Constantly feeling unappreciated.

6. Lacks contentment.

7. Depressed to any degree.

8. Highly defensive without just cause.

9. When faced with challenges, responds with, "I can't" or "I don't know how to."

10. Has a harsh personal self-view or is critical of themselves.

It is important to note that all the above behaviors are steeped in manipulation of some form or another. If your child exhibits more than five of these behaviors, there's a good chance the victim spirit is a root that needs to be dealt with in a very direct and consistent matter. Like I mentioned before, we all have bad days, so anyone of us can exhibit any of these inappropriate behaviors here and there. However, even the limited times need to be dealt with swiftly. If any of these descriptions describe your child, there is an even greater urgency to eradicate this destructive mindset and behavior.

There is a higher level of discernment that needs to arise within your person to commit to finding out what could be causing the victim spirit to reside within your child's psyche. This would be a good time to set aside calendar space to have one-on-one time to ask your child some questions. During your one-on-one, make sure you provide a safe place for your child to be open and honest with you to share what is on their heart. They should be able to share any concerns or fears they have with you.

Always make sure you ask them if there is anything you need to know that they haven't been telling you. While the victim mindset can be triggered by traumatic situations, many times it's a learned attribute—in other words, generational thinking. I have noted that many families have generations with the victim spirit or mindset. It is passed down from member to member until someone breaks the chains! In adults, it's often coupled with clinical or cyclical depression. However, I have wonderful news! This is not a lifelong sentence. There is hope! I have seen many adults and children overcome such generational bonds and live as victors, not victims!

While it is true that some children and adults have been truly victimized, the important factor to remember is that they do not have to live as victims. The goal for a survivor is to be a victor, from victim to victory! Giving our children tools for conquering such a mindset has an everlasting value. The day I began this chapter, I had a child showing signs of the broken victim mindset. It's now easy for me to identify which kids have a predisposition to it since it is a generational pattern.

My husband is a hard worker and a loving dad, but crushing this mindset is something he had to master over a long period of time. Praise God, he conquered it. Yes, he got victory over this spirit that has manifested in so much of his extended family. I only mention this to make a point to show the generational link which means kids don't have to experience trauma to exhibit such behavior.

Some of my kids have dealt with this spirit/mindset even though they have had a very protected and intentional upbringing. I have done my best to cherish and nurture them from the time they were born, yet the generational tie can be powerful.

Getting back to the child who was having "one of those days," I could see that something was wrong, and finally, I asked her, and she admitted she knew what was going on. I asked her how I could help her, and she said, "Just pray for me. I know I am having a struggle emotionally today, and I know I shouldn't believe lies." She went down the list of thoughts she identified as problem thinking. Basically, she just needed some spiritual support through prayer and motivational talk. I asked my little boys today about what the victim spirit looks like when in action their lives, and they each had their own response. Here are some of their own words: "No one wants to play with me, no one appreciates me; I can't do anything right." They each mentioned a negative mindset process that happens. However, I was so encouraged because my eleven-year-old told me, "I'm over it now. This is a new year, and I am going to rule my emotions." He said it in a very confident and sure voice. Victory!

# Take Action

Two things I learned about the Victim Mindset:

_____

_____

_____

_____

Which signs stuck out to you the most?

_____

_____

_____

What will you begin to practice at home to keep the Victim

Mindset in check?

_____

_____

_____

_____

_____

_____

# The 4 Non-Negotiables

In my experience, we need to set some very clear ground rules in the following four areas to promote a healthy relationship with our children.

### The 4 Non-Negotiables

1. Respect
2. Manipulation
3. Lying
4. Gratefulness

Each of these topics is in the non-negotiable category. This means our kids should not try to negotiate with us on them under any circumstance. Over the years after counseling so many moms, I found that many of them struggle to identify when their kids are behaving disrespectfully towards them. It seems that onlookers can see it, but they are missing it.

I suggest before reading the next four steps in the subcategories that you take time to pray and ask Yahweh to give you eyes to see and ears to hear the message exactly how you need to receive it. Let His Spirit be your guide.

# Prayer

Lord, here I am, mold me, shape me. Create in me a pure heart. Renew a right spirit within me. Open my spiritual eyes, ears and heart to the things of your Spirit, Father. Bind the strongman that has kept me from seeing areas that I need to surrender to you. Empower me and embolden me to do your will. In Yeshua's name, amen.

# Respect

Over the years, I have repeatedly witnessed kids disrespecting their parents by backtalking, which I characterize as "average" or common behavior. Mama, if you want to raise kids who will change the world, your kids must respect those in authority—especially you! It's important to acknowledge that raising kids to be "average" doesn't set them up to enter the 1 percent category of society. I don't know about you, but I want my kids to be financially and emotionally free when they become adults.

Mama, you are here. So I am assuming you have accepted the mandate to be a Mother of Change. If you have, I know you want your kids to grow up to change the world and be in the 1 percent of success stories! If you desire to reach higher for your family, flee from living an "average" lifestyle because it is equal to living "lukewarm."

---

*So then because thou art lukewarm, and neither cold nor hot, I will spue thee out of my mouth. Rev. 3:16*

---

If the road to destruction is wide and the way to salvation is narrow, I desire the narrow way. (Math. 7:13-14)

*Even so then at this present time also there is a **remnant** according to the election of grace. Rom. 11:5*

---

*Remnant defined: a usually small part, member, or trace remaining*
*(Merriam-Webster)*

---

I have no desire to raise my kids like the majority that is living according to the flesh. I always want to stay in the minority or remnant that is focused on living by the spirit.

Average behavior does not contain righteous, salty flavor, or fortitude.

- "Average" describes kids and people in society who have no desire to be consecrated or separated unto God. They seek to fulfill the lusts of their flesh rather than to live by the Spirit. In short, they seek *pleasure over purpose.*

Let me make this clear: kids who disrespect their parents are on the wide road that leads to destruction! If you are allowing your kids to sass you and be disrespectful toward you or your husband, stop it and shut that behavior down. Yahweh has commanded your kids to honor you, and that is the bottom line. I have always made sure my kids respect my husband and their elders. I have zero tolerance for disrespect.

Remember, you're not doing your kids any favors by allowing such behavior. Instead, you are handicapping them spiritually.

*And whosoever shall exalt himself shall be abased; and he that shall humble himself shall be exalted. Matt. 23:12*

You are setting them up for a hard fall because the Father abases the proud!

*Abase- to lower in rank, office, prestige, or esteem. (Merriam-webster)*

He will humble them until they repent, and then He will raise them up! And, if they don't repent, woe to them. We want our kids to honor God's Word and us. The great news is that when they are honoring us, it comes with the blessing of a long life.

Honor your father and your mother, as the Lord your God has commanded you, that *your days may be long*, and that it may be well with you in the land which the Lord your God is giving you. (Deut. 5:26)

Let me encourage you to concentrate on being a mom that is worthy of admiration and respect.

- Do you want your kids to look up to you? Require their respect.
- Do you want them to take you seriously? Don't allow them to respond to you with pride in their hearts.

Kids don't call the shots. If your kids are making all the decisions, you are giving them way too much power. It's one thing to have their input in a group discussion as long they understand that Mom and Dad have the final say.

If you give your kid permission to act like a dictator, he or she will no matter how young they are. Don't lie to yourself; you're not cultivating good character by allowing excess liberty in your home. Maybe your child is showing good character, but trust me, it's not the allowance of extreme liberty that bears this kind of fruit. After you have multiple children, the reality sets in real quick that they are all created unique. Each child has a different temperament. Every so often, there is that great child that makes us feel like we are doing a great job at parenting. However, the next child shows us it wasn't really our parenting style, after all! I have had the wakeup call even in my own home! Here I was taking credit for something that was due to God's grace in my life. Talk about being humbled.

Some moms might read this section and feel the guilt try to sneak in, reject it! Don't take on shame, instead change your direction in parenting by acknowledging areas that require a shift. Make sure to do it without letting the enemy take you down emotionally. Practice the following four steps to free yourself to grow.

## 4 STEPS TO THAT LEAD TO RESPECT:

1. Repent.
2. Forgive yourself.
3. Course correct.
4. Stay on the right track.

If you get off track, repeat the steps and course correct as the Spirit leads. When dealing with disrespect, remember the worst offenders in our society lack respect. They lack respect for authority, for humanity and God. It's a severe offense to consider. The question is, how serious is disrespect to you now that you have read this section?

# Take Action

What would you currently rate the respect level of your kids toward you and your husband? (Scale 1-10)

_____

What are the 4-non negotiables?

_____

_____

_____

_____

What are 4 steps to take when you make a parenting or personal mistake?

_____

_____

_____

_____

_____

_____

# Manipulation

Manipulation is like a dirty word in my house. I teach my kids at an early age that we have a zero-tolerance policy for it. The first time a kid tries to manipulate usually is one of the last times unless they are brave enough to try it again. I remember when my son was around eight years old, and he tried the whole manipulation thing. He came to me and asked if he could do something, and I said no. Then he went outside and to his dad and asked the same question. My husband said yes. Well, when my husband found out what our son did, he put his foot down quick-like! He pulled my son aside and told him, "Don't you ever manipulate me again! When your mama tells you something, you don't come to me looking for another answer because that is called manipulation, and that is never going to fly in our home! My wife will be with me long after you leave the nest, and you will not put enmity between us by causing division in our home!" This day was memorable in our home, but my son got the point. If you are a single mama, maybe you are allowing manipulation out of guilt because you feel like your kids have been through so much already, but don't ever allow guilt to steer your decisions with your kids. Address the issue with your child by asking yourself if he or she is taking advantage of you!

If the answer is yes, remember, your child is taking advantage of your soft spot, and he or she is working you over! Don't put up with it! Let your yes be yes, and your no

161

be a no! When your kid is persistent in trying to break you down, take swift action! Don't make your consequence small either, especially if they are continually whining for something. My kids know better than to complain to me because I teach them young that whining gets them nothing but a consequence with me. It's fruitless. Kids have a way of processing things: If I do this.... I get this...

How are you training your kids? And, I am not just talking about the little kids either? As moms, we teach our kids how to treat us. Remember, we talked about requiring honor at the very beginning of this book. If you allow them to push you over, they will and without guilt.

Personally, we shut down whining immediately in our home. Even my teens will shut down a little brother if they hear him acting up with a sibling. *Remember, manipulation is a character fail.* Manipulators are self-focused and are willing to bend the truth to get their way. When we identify behavior that is counter to the Word, we need to steer our kids back on the path of righteousness because it's the right thing to do. It's the *"God thing"* to do because lying or flattering speech is never mentioned as positive communication in the Bible.

---

*For those who are such do not serve our Lord Jesus Christ, but their own belly, and by smooth words and flattering speech deceive the hearts of the simple. (Rom. 16:18)*

---

When your kid is using this unholy tool to get his or her way, use this opportunity for leveraging. If they were manipulating to get more time to play video games, then make the removal of the object their consequence. Let them know they were looking for more time to play, but their plan backfired. This can also be the point where you identify if the child has an addiction to video games. Whenever a person puts an object or thing over a relationship, there is usually an unhealthy mindset or obsession at hand.

If they are manipulating to visit a friend, this could be indicative of a soul-tie that needs to be broken. Soul ties can cause kids to make reckless decisions. I can remember when I was fourteen; I formed a soul-tie with my best friend. Because of her influence in my life, I took my first drink, tried drugs, skipped school, got into boys, and I got into a ton of trouble until I finally got kicked out of school! It was the hardest time of my teenage years for sure. However, being expelled turned out to be the best thing that could happen to me. My mom put me on restriction from hanging out with my best friend, and I wasn't around my high school peers for months. During my homeschool semester, I used an academic program through my local high school, and it was then that I got my head straight. I broke off that soul-tie with her and seen the situation for what it was. I realized that she was causing me to get in trouble. I also realized I was trying to fit in too hard, and I put a stop to it all. I went back to school ready to excel, ready to prove to myself that I didn't need cliques or people to be popular. I went on to be voted onto A.S.B., our Associated Student Body. I also got voted onto the homecoming court, and I won a spot in our yearbook for a vain title that I won't even mention.

What changed for me? First of all, my mom put her foot down and put a serious fear in me, serious. But, more importantly, the school's decision was the most impacting. They kicked me out of school, and it was the gamechanger. My mom would have never thought of homeschooling me. She was only fourteen when she had me, which made her only twenty-nine when I started getting into trouble. I am pretty sure she didn't consider herself qualified to school me. As a matter of fact, I remember her looking into other high schools to send me to for the semester. I can only imagine the trouble I would have gotten myself into being the new kid in school. I am so very glad she didn't.

God has a way of coordinating things in our life, according to His plan. My homeschool was basic. I did workbook work and turned my assignments into school proctors to check weekly. I kept on track, and my mom didn't have to worry about teaching me. If you are at a crossroads with your child and you are sensing that public school or even private school is not a safe place for your child for whatever reason, homeschooling isn't difficult. It's only as hard as you make it.

If your child is getting in trouble at school, and you need to act quick, there are online state homeschool programs you can use to bring them home. This means they will learn the same things other students are learning in school but from home. Don't forget; I didn't keep my kids home for academic reasons. I kept them home to protect them, period. So, I never worried about my qualifications. I wanted to protect them from others and themselves. I wanted to curb them from making dumb decisions they would regret later like I did. When I think of all the dumb things I did when I was younger, I realize those same mistakes today could lead to serious danger, especially with trafficking on the rise. So back to manipulation, you have decisions and options to consider.

If your kid is using manipulation and you connect it to influence from their peer group, I would suggest weighing out your options deeply and by prayer. When things or people repeatedly come between your relationship with your kids, take action to remove the offenders from your family's life, if not for good then for a good long time if possible. It will give them time to think about the poor decision they made. I have made this decision on more than one occasion, and I can say that my kids have always come around to thank me for my decision to separate them from friendships that had soul-ties. Whatever you decide, make sure to stick to what you say, and prayerfully your kids begin to trust that you will do what you say you will! Remaining true to your word will impact your kids in the present and, by prayer, bear good fruit in the future.

# Take Action

How would your kid/s answer this question?

If I whine long and loud enough, I get...

_____

_____

Do your kids use manipulation as a tool to get their way?

_____

_____

What is your plan to change things?

_____

_____

When things or people come between your relationship with your kids you should do what?

_____

_____

_____

_____

_____

# Lying

Let's go back to the garden of Eden. What was the original sin? Wasn't it disobedience when Adam and Eve ignored Yahweh's commands and believed a lie?

I tell my kids that lying isn't only defined as giving the wrong information. It is also purposely withholding information to keep from getting in trouble, and it includes sharing only half of a story with an ulterior motive!

## ABOUT LYING

- Kids must understand lying in any form can't be tolerated.
- Exaggeration and embellishing stories are forms of lying too.
- Lying is loathsome, and God hates it. How do I know He hates it? Because scriptures says so!

---

*Lying lips are an abomination to the Lord, But those who deal truthfully are His delight. (Prov. 12:22)*
*A righteous man hates lying. (Prov. 13:5)*
*Six things does the Lord hate and one of them is lying! (Prov. 6:16-19)*

---

If I hear a kid embellishing or adding extra information to a story or giving information as though it is a fact without knowing for sure, I correct them immediately. I consider this entry-level lying, and it's not okay. If my kids are sharing info they are unsure of, I have them use the phrase, "I think," before continuing. Lying is not always blatant, and it enters in the smallest ways. The enemy is crafty at getting a kid to sear their conscience. So be on guard of that kind of behavior. Make sure you are a good example to your kids in this area as well.

## 2 PRINCIPALS ABOUT LYING

1. Gossip can beget lies.
   o Steer clear from gossip and hearsay to avoid getting wrapped up with half-truths, which can add up to lies.
2. People who lie can't be trusted.
   o People who lie in small matters will lie in the weightier ones.

Kids who lie need to be monitored highly, and that is not fun for anyone.

Just this week, I was watching a social media video compilation that showed toddler after toddler caught doing things they weren't supposed to, and each time they got caught they lied!

Little Johnny, did you eat the candy?

No, I didn't eat the candy.

Then what's that blue stuff all over your mouth?

You probably get the picture.

Mama, it's easy to laugh at such situations but remember what you allow when they are little will only flourish as they grow older. Do your best to curb this character flaw early in their life by being an active listener. Watch for embellishments, and do not enable lying at any level.

# Take Action

Lying can also include:

_____

_____

_____

Do you have any level of lying going on in your house?

_____

_____

How does that make you feel?

_____

_____

_____

What is your goal this week to keep you sensitive to lying?

_____

_____

_____

Finish this sentence: People who lie can't be _____.

_____

_____

# Gratefulness

In a society where parents have accepted materialism by constantly buying their kids the latest and greatest, it's no wonder kids lack gratefulness. The lack of this virtue contributes to a decaying world.

## Gratefulness is the foundation of a healthy community and home.

Where there is a deficit in gratitude weeds of selfishness + idleness + disharmony + entitlement will grow!

Ungrateful weeds pop up as:

1.  Lazy.
2.  Arrogant.
3.  Rude.
4.  Victim attitude.
a.  "Life isn't fair."
5.  Never satisfied.

Cultivating gratefulness in your child is only done through intentional parenting. You can't just tell a kid to be grateful and expect it to happen. Instead, act as if you are planting a garden. You must plow up the soil of his or her heart first and break up the fallow ground before you ever plant the seed! Fallow ground is hard ground that needs to be broken up to plant a productive garden. It's no different from people who have hard hearts or have developed rebellion.

There's a certain amount of work that must take place to soften up a person's heart to receive new things.

---

*Then He spoke many things to them in parables, saying: "Behold, a sower went out to sow. And as he sowed, some seed fell by the wayside; and the birds came and devoured them. Some fell on stony places, where they did not have much earth; and they immediately sprang up because they had no depth of earth. But when the sun was up they were scorched, and because they had no root they withered away. And some fell among thorns, and the thorns sprang up and choked them. But others fell on good ground and yielded a crop: some a hundredfold, some sixty, some thirty. He who has ears to hear, let him hear! (Matt. 13:3-9)*

---

Scripture indicates the importance of the condition of the "soil," which is an analogy of the heart. Early on in my marriage, I can clearly remember the Spirit showing me that my husband and I were plowers. In gardening, plowers go out with a plow and break up the hard, compacted dirt before sowing seed. It can be extremely labor-intensive. I can remember thinking to myself, "Plower? I would love to be a harvester!" For many years we would "plow" in someone's life, and then the Father would move us onward to another field. It was always laborious work emotionally and spiritually, but we knew it was necessary. I see now the Lord used those years of training to prepare me to handle tilling my children's hearts. Gratefulness must be cultivated. Most of the time, it must be planted in a child's heart.

So, talk about gratefulness in your home and set up habits for the family to practice this positive character trait. Have a heart check time with your family regularly. Check out my Created for Change Journal that includes writing prompts to help you cultivate a positive mindset and gratefulness.

If at any point you notice your children developing an attitude of entitlement, it is time to step back and start allowing some struggle in their lives. You may want to take away some creature comforts too! Ungratefulness shouldn't be tolerated. While you can't make a kid be grateful, you can provide an atmosphere for them to learn this virtue by keeping them accountable and not giving into manipulation. When they receive things, make sure they show appreciation.

My kids are known for their grateful attitudes, but they weren't born with that attitude. We have worked hard to make sure they understand the importance of showing gratefulness to others, especially when they are shown favor or given gifts. If I even sense they are not visually showing enough gratefulness when others are blessing them, I address it with them privately one hundred percent of the time. I don't let it slip. As I was raising my first set of kids, I made sure to provide opportunities for them to learn about hard lifestyles. So, I used to take them with me to a women's shelter to volunteer cleaning, and we provided needs for the women. Of course, if you are going to take your kids with you to do community ministry, make sure to keep them close by! Don't let your eyes off of them.

Later, when I had my second set of kids, we were actually living in a destitute situation ourselves. We lived in the middle of nowhere, without electricity or running water! Times were tough, but I wouldn't trade that season for anything! If you want your kids to be grateful for floors without holes, running water, and shoes that fit, let them experience some lack for a season. Something we did to broaden our kid's scope of the world was to watch documentaries of families living in third world countries etc. After we finished watching the movies, we would have a full family discussion. We talk a lot in our home. I believe good communication is the strength of a family. So, make time weekly to have family talks.

During that time, remind them of their many blessings.

RECAP ON CULTIVATING GRATEFULNESS:

1. Provide opportunities for them to learn about hard lifestyles.
2. Let them experience some lack or struggle.
3. Watch documentaries of people groups living in poverty to cultivate gratefulness.
4. Have stimulating conversations after each experience or opportunity.

An attitude of gratitude is a lifestyle habit that must not be neglected if you desire to raise kids who will be the hope for our future.

Gratitude is a home stabilizer, never forget that.

# Take Action

If I were to rate the gratefulness level in my kids I would give them a number rating of: (Scale 1-10) _____.

Now that you answered the above question. Ask Yahweh what He rates your children. Pray and wait for His response. Record it here:

_____

_____

_____

Finish this statement: Gratitude is a home _____.

_____

_____

How can you cultivate gratitude in your home?

_____

_____

_____

**Remember, an attitude of gratitude**

**will act as an anchor through the worst storms of life.**

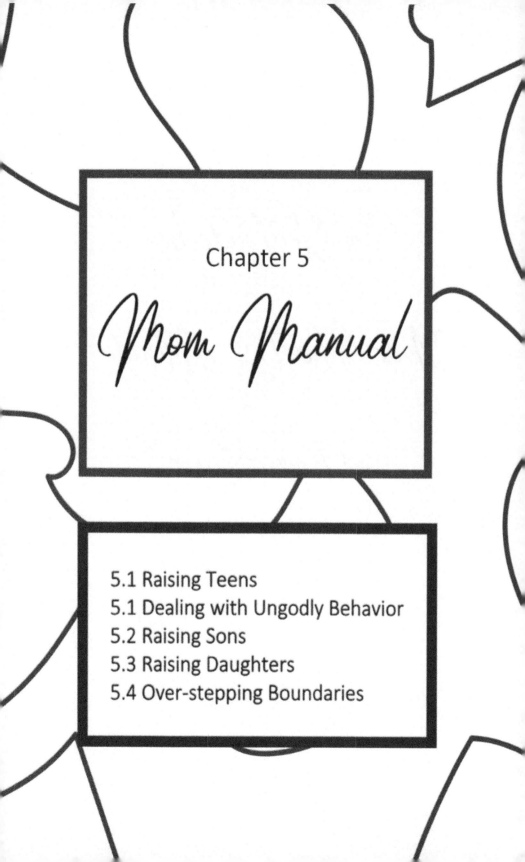

Chapter 5

*Mom Manual*

Let Gratitude be

Your Heart,s Attitude

-EmmaSara

# Raising Teens

Teens today are often described as self-indulgent, detached, social media-addicted humans. I can't tell you how many times I heard about how terrible the teen years would be. The regular comment was, "You have how many kids? Oh, wait until they become teens!" As if it was a season in life to be dreaded. While I can understand why I heard the caution so many times based upon the common teen experience, I can officially say that one of my daughters is completely through her teen years, and it was a beautiful time for me as a parent. My oldest son just turned eighteen last month, and I really enjoy him. My biggest issue with him is that he is incredibly forgetful, and because of his personality type, he is a debater to the core, which can be irritating at times. So, I am not saying my kids are perfect. However, just because they are not flawless doesn't make this stage miserable. My second daughter is sixteen, and she can exhibit some common teen tendencies, but I am able to be a big influence in her life still. As a matter of fact, she is a lot like me. I will say that our good relationship didn't happen by accident. It took a lot of forethought and strategy over the years.

Two main areas that I focused on were cultivating both trust and respect. The basis for creating this foundation is found in the 4 Non-Negotiables. As a mom of teens, I can say it is such a relief that they trust my judgment, and they can confide in me a lot, which is huge for a parent-teen relationship. Part of that trust comes from not over-reacting when they open up about personal issues. Overly emotional parents can push a teen away when they are trying to be transparent with their personal struggles. It's common for some parents to react to information and go into lecture mode, but this causes kids to clam up and withhold information. In situations where I can sense that there are deep issues that need to be dealt with, I go into listener mode. There are plenty of times I don't listen well in life, but I made a resolve early on in marriage to be a safe place for my kids and my husband to share their temptations with me.

Creating an environment for transparency is a very delicate area, so I make myself resilient and prepared to hear the worst and hope for the best. This method allows me to stage the conversation to be a safe zone. However, one mistake I often see that is common with raising teens is when a mom acts like a peer when their teens open up. Some parents feel like it's either/or, to lecture or to be a friend, so they choose to be a friend over a potential enemy. However, it shouldn't be either or because alone; each is a poor strategy for raising resilient, mature teens. Being aware of spiritual influences in your kid's life is going to be pivotal in keeping his or her heart. Be in tune with the Holy Spirit so you can see life as God sees it. Sometimes we get so busy doing the daily grind that we forget we are here to glorify God and serve Him forever. We forget that we are supposed to be making sure spiritual invaders haven't crept in. So it's important to tap into God through prayer and seek Him in all your ways, and He will direct your parenting path.

Another way to gain your teen's heart is to teach them to tap into their life calling. It's the perfect age to help them press into further developing their God-given talents. Remember, you can help a child identify their gift by assisting them to recognize what's easy for them but hard for most others. A lot of times, we go through autopilot in life just living and being without realizing something is truly a gift endowed to us by God. When we succeed in connecting our kids with their purpose, watch out because they will begin to bloom and bloom! I can say with confidence that this method has kept my young adults loyal to us because we support them in fulfilling their dreams according to their God-given talents. In my book, Passion. Purpose. Time Management. I give a partial workbook format to assist you in determining the difference between a passion and a true life calling in life. Sometimes things we are passionate about are not truly a calling. Understanding that is imperative when helping your kids identify their calling. Remember to always seek the Lord for insight in this very important area. He wants to reveal the answer to you. He wants to make it clear if you press into Him and lay your perceived desires at His feet. Sometimes what we want is not what we need in our life.

# Prayer

Father in heaven, hallowed be thy name. Thy kingdom come, thy will be done in my life and my children's life. Let it be done on earth as it is in heaven. Lord, show me your perfect will for my kid's life. Open up revelation in a clear way. Reveal your plan to my family about the path you would have us take to build a family legacy. In Yeshua's name, amen.

# How to Deal with Ungodly Behavior

At some point, our kids will act out to some degree and show ungodly behavior. When that happens, it's good to be prepared. A strategy is everything in such circumstances. Over the years, I have developed a proven strategy that has kept my kid's heart towards me while conquering much.

**Here is your Warrior Queen Strategy breakdown to deal with ungodly behavior and the secret to communicating effectively with your kids.** *(I suggest keeping this list handy!)*

### Part 1 Strategy: Create a safe place.

1. Approach the situation after you have prayed for a strategy.
2. Pray for your child to be open to the voice of God in their own lives.
3. Find a private place to talk and go in with the frame of mind that you are going to provide a safe place for them to be transparent.
4. After they open up, do not lecture, shame, yell, cry, or use emotions.

5. Counsel them with the truth of God's word and use affirmations to speak over them. Speak about who they are in God. Counsel them to identify the enemy working in their life, by asking questions rather than telling them what they need to know.

It's very important to concentrate on the character issue at hand, rather than the isolated event. Most people deal with the event and don't focus on the root character flaw.

**Here are the top root causes of kids acting out:**

1. Pride
2. Envy
3. Selfishness
4. Lust
5. Greed

**Part 2 Strategy: The art of asking questions.**

This strategy has proven to be extremely powerful in getting to root issues. The great part is that my kids are the ones that access themselves. Let them tell you what they know about their situation.

1. Did you know that you were about to make the wrong choice?
2. How did you feel after you did it?
3. Did you hear the voice of God when you were doing it?
4. What did He tell you?
5. Did you hear any voices?
6. What would have been a better decision?
7. Do you wish you did something different?
8. Who have you hurt?

9. Which of God's laws have you violated?
10. Do you think you were acting out in _____? Name 1 of the 5 sinful roots or whatever the Spirit shows you.
11. Do you want to repent to God?
12. What do you think your consequence should be?
13. What are you going to do to prevent yourself from making that same mistake in the future?
14. How can I help you or protect you from the enemy's attack?

This list is by no means exhaustive. I rely on being Spirit lead to ask questions. I watch their body language, and I have an ear to the Lord. I sit listening to my child, and with the other ear, I am listening for the voice of God. After I ask a series of questions that helps to usher in a breakthrough, I help them stay in the moment.

When a son or daughter gains personal insight, it's a huge victory for our kids. When you can lead your child to a safe place and help them to work things out for themselves, simply by asking the right questions, it's a powerful relational tool to build trust. I involve them in personal discovery, and then involve them in setting up a consequence. They still need to be held accountable for their decision. If you got to their heart, they would agree they need one. There will be times you will name the consequence, but as much as possible, I let them choose it. If I choose the reprimand, it normally correlates with the action. If they crossed a boundary with the computer, that means it will be taken away for a while. However, when your kids commits an offense and creates the consequence, there is greater ownership and a higher level of

185

accountability, and this helps preserve your relationship. Of course, if they choose something easy or that's not really a consequence, address that issue.

**Part 3 Strategy: Close with the power of the Holy Spirit.**

1. Make sure to speak against the spiritual principalities. Stake your claim over your child. Tell satan to flee because you obey Yeshua and His word says that the enemy must flee! Have your kid say it too.
2. End your time with them, letting your child know how much you love them and thank them for opening up.
3. Find a Bible scripture to strengthen them and ask them to get alone with God and write it out and write out what they learned. When they are done, have them share their entry with you.
4. Lastly, DO NOT MAKE excuses for their sin.

Do not take the blame for their bad decisions. Don't gloss it over, don't pass it by, and don't think that if you were nicer, they wouldn't have their issues. Poor choices are always a personal accountability issue. Sinful behavior is never ok anytime or anywhere—not in the workplace, at school, or anywhere. If the Lord shows you to change something in your parenting, do so, but don't ever make your shortcoming an excuse for their sinful behavior.

Part of successful teen communication comes forth by encouraging them to develop their own personal godly convictions. As parents, we can't force our convictions on them. They must develop their own faith and take ownership of their walk with God. Gaining their heart and their respect is the key to building a strong relationship that can weather any storm. I have had the privilege of working through teen hurdles with my kids repeatedly, and each time I have secured their trust and respect. There is an art of communication when dealing with kids, and when you learn it, it is worth its weight in gold.

# Take Action

Two strategies that I need to adopt to handle ungodly behavior:

_____

_____

One area that brought a personal conviction concerning dealing with hard issues is:

_____

_____

I will act in this area of conviction by:

_____

_____

_____

What have you learned about communicating with your kids in this chapter?

_____

_____

_____

# Raising Sons

As a mother of six sons, the topic of raising boys is near and dear to my heart. In a nation where feminism is continually on the rise and gender, neutrality is now entering the schools; there has never been a more important time in history to take back ground in the area of raising sons! On the topic of feminism, I am not alluding that women shouldn't be strong or have a voice because if you have come this far in the book, you probably realize that I am not a weak woman. With that said, I am embarrassed to admit I have made some huge mistakes in my early years of parenting. I allowed the mindset of the world to cloud my judgment when I was first raising my sons. I coddled him and wanted him to be gentle. I didn't let him wrestle with boys because I thought it was too aggressive even though his friends just wanted to play and have fun, as most boys do. The bottom line is that we fed passivity to him. I used to say that he didn't have to do the stereotypical things that boys did because I wanted him to be confident in his manhood without the stereotype. In reality, I was saying I wanted him to feel confident in his masculinity while not acting masculine! It's insanity. It doesn't make sense, and this is why satan is the author of confusion. Why did I start to raise my son in such a way? Because I was buying into a feminizing culture! Gratefully, I figured out what I was inviting into my home through prayer.

God opened my eyes and showed me some poor fruit that was manifesting from raising him in such a way.

I feel like we had to step back with him to erase and reconstruct the definition of what it is to be masculine and strong. Based on the different color personality tests we have taken, I realize that not all men have the same personality type; every man is unique. I understand that some guys are strong leaders, while others are more peaceable and less decisive. Some men don't even like to lead. I realize that aggression doesn't define masculinity. Understanding a man's responsibilities to society and the family is what helps to define a real man. Teaching strong gender identity, rather than confusion, is the focus. Some boys need to be taught about initiative and protection, while some are natural protectors and leaders.

So I'm not overlooking a boy's natural bents or traits, instead it's a shift in focus. It's about cultivating godliness and chivalry in our sons. Once upon a time, our men were trained to let women and children go first to safety when lives were at stake amid trouble. However, there have been some more recent shameful stories of captains who left their ships to seek safety while women and children were still trying to exit a sinking ship! It's a sad day when there is such a confusion in society that children suffer and are put into unsafe situations because some men are cowards and disrespectful of God's order.

There is such a present gender confusion in society that it makes me wonder how certain safety situations would play out if some men considered themselves female. Can you

192

imagine the big guy in the dress displacing your daughter in the safety boat because he arrived there first? After all, it is females and children first, right?

Now, let's look at another scenario in a current setting and imagine a woman and her thirteen-year-old daughter are shopping at a neighborhood store. Suddenly, a man reaches out and grabs the young girl and starts dragging her out of the store violently! The mom jumps into action to grab hold of her daughter, but the crazed man keeps pulling her daughter through the store like a rag doll! Can you imagine this guy was brazen enough to do this act during broad daylight in a popular store? The situation escalates as the mom was gripping onto her daughter for dear life. The struggle continues as the girl is slid around a corner when something shocking happens! A young man jumps out of the way as the kidnapper slides the girl past the onlooker! He did nothing to physically help the mom in her tug of war for her daughter. His inaction could have allowed this young girl to be abducted! This sounds ludicrous, right? Well, this is a true story[11] of what happens when men lose the drive to protect women and children as the weaker vessels.

As I was reading the comments under the video, I noted a comment that mentioned that women can protect themselves, as if a man shouldn't protect a woman being brutalized by a man. Gratefully there was an off-duty police officer outside that captured the aggressor, and the girl was safe, thank the Lord.

It's madness. It's a satanic mindset that would state that men should be neutral when it comes to stepping in to defend and protect women and children. Identify the evil mindset and stand against it. Do not partner with it.

Mama, teach your son to be strong and also teach him to be a gentleman. I know some women don't want a door opened for them but encourage your son to at least offer.

(My six sons)

Just last night, my husband and I were out eating dinner, and a man came up to our table and looked at my husband and said, "I noticed you pulling your chair out for your wife. You don't see that anymore." He was pleased to see my husband honoring me. Moms don't do everything for your son. Have him do things for you. If he sees you carrying something, he should hop up to help you. Enabling our sons only creates handicap men. We aren't doing them any favors with this kind of behavior. It is disturbing to me that this generation is riddled with demasculinized men.

They are effeminate, which is defined

(1) having feminine qualities untypical of a man: not manly in appearance or manner, and (2) marked by an unbecoming delicacy or over-refinement" (Merriam Webster.)

Just recently, I went shopping, and I felt unsettled that clothes are now being marketed as gender-neutral. I found myself looking items over, noting that they were too girly to put on boys and too masculine to put on girls! I found the same shirts in both the girls' and boys' sections to prove my point! I have been having a hard time finding my son's pants that don't look feminine, and I don't like it. I am not raising girlish boys. I am raising mighty men of valor, and I make sure to remind them of that daily! God will use them. They will be gentlemen, and they will treat women with respect and view them as a weaker vessel as it states in scripture.

Husbands, likewise, dwell with them with understanding, giving honor to the wife, as to the weaker vessel, and as being heirs together of the grace of life, that your prayers may not be hindered. (1 Pet. 3:7)

The Greek translation for weak is to "make or manufacture." Vessel speaks of something that contains liquid, like a water pitcher.

So my view is that a woman is manufactured/created to pour out a pure blessing, so she should be treated with respect and honor.

When it comes to adversity, I want my boys to respond as protectors.

---

*"Let us be strong for our people and for the cities of our God." (2 Sam. 10:12).*

---

(My oldest son during PT)

I am entirely unashamed to raise sons who will be confident in their manhood.

Even with all that I have mentioned, I would like to make it clear that I have adult friends and family members who have chosen a gay lifestyle. I admit I don't agree with their lifestyle, but nor do I agree with heterosexual couples living together unmarried either. So, this book is not written to shame or to be hateful to people with alternative lifestyles. However, if any person tries to indoctrinate my kids to live contrary to the Bible or hurt them, they will have to deal with this lioness mom. Adults can make decisions for themselves, and I am not trying to get involved in their lifestyle choices unless it involves a kid's safety or trying to sway my family away from Biblical living.

Praying to develop Spirit lead convictions and standards to protect our families is important. Remember, the enemy is anti-God, and he is looking to indoctrinate our kids with the ways of the world at every level. So, why are we allowing our kids to wear "gender-neutral" clothes from clothing lines that are purposely trying to blur the lines between male and female with the sole purpose of confusing them about their sexuality?

Where are the Warrior Moms who will say, "Not on my watch!"

Mama, if you have sons, let us join in raising mighty men of valor who will uphold God's ways in society.

---

*Then one of the servants answered and said, "Look, I have seen a son of Jesse the Bethlehemite, who is skillful in playing, a mighty man of valor, a man of war, prudent in speech, and a handsome person; and the Lord is with him." (1 Sam. 16:18)*

*The man Jeroboam was a mighty man of valor; and Solomon, seeing that the young man was industrious, made him the officer over all the labor force of the house of Joseph. (1 Kings 11:28)*

---

Mama, can I ask you a question? Where are you getting your instructions for raising a son? Are you taking directions from the same world that is trying to feminize boys, or from the Word? What does the Bible instruct us to teach them? We should raise them to be mighty men of valor, industrious, skillful, prudent in speech, and fearless men in any battle.

(Boys doing push-ups)

Just like we as women get instruction from Proverbs 31, our sons should get their guidance from scripture too.

What else does the Bible say about raising kids?

---

*"Train up a child in the way he should go, And when he is old he will not depart from it." (Prov. 22:6)*

---

If you live by the Word, then you can stand by it. You can proclaim it over your children! There is power in the name of Yeshua/Jesus, so use it over your children when proclaiming the promises of God!

Is your child facing gender confusion? For the sake of humanity and their sanity and soul—don't feed it! Get to the root and battle in the spirit. Repent for any doors you allowed to be opened and take back ground!

Remember, foolishness is bound up in the heart of a child, according to Proverbs 22:15!

The Greek transliteration for foolishness is "ivveleth" or "evil!" The translation for heart is "inner man," "mind," or "will."

So with the transliterations and translations, Proverbs 22:15 could be read like this, "Evil is bound up in the mind and will of the child, but the staff of correction and discipline will remove it far from him."

*Don't believe the lie that your young child knows what is best for them.*

Satan wants your child, so be on guard!

*Train your child up in the way he should go, or the world will be happy to do it for you!*

# Take Action

What defines a real man?

_____

_____

_____

My heart was convicted in this area:

_____

_____

What is the definition of effeminate?

_____

Fill in the blank. I need to train up my child in the way he
should go or the _____ will be happy to do it for
me.

_____

How does the Bible describe Godly men?

_____

_____

_____

# Raising Daughters

We have the ability to raise daughters of change, change for society. I have two daughters. My oldest is twenty, and my second daughter will be seventeen in two short months. I know it sounds so cliché, but it really feels like they were little girls just yesterday. As I was raising my girls, I was extremely focused on raising maidens (young women) of virtue, which meant I had to have a strategy in place. I purposed to raise them counter to popular culture. So, I was continually seeking God and the Word for my gameplan.

I had to decide what I wanted to raise my girls with and without. I didn't raise my girls with barbies or princess stories. Princess stories were fabrications of what would never be, and I didn't want to set them up to have false expectations when they got married. The fact is no one is perfect, and Prince Charming doesn't exist except in the minds of disillusioned girls and women. After years of counseling women, I found there was a common theme of shattered dreams among wives because they expected their husbands to live up to the prince charming fantasy. And, let's not forget that Cinderella doesn't really describe any woman we know either.

I didn't buy barbies for my girls because they represented a secular culture, and I didn't want my girls to get a false perception of what their bodies were supposed to look like. Besides, I remember my dolls "acting adultish," which sparked a desire within me to grow up too early, and I wanted my daughters to enjoy their youth. So you could definitely say that I was extremely intentional in my parenting style. One thing that is important to mention is that although I was focused on raising counter-culture kids, I never wanted to be a strict parent.

A couple of years ago, I remember a new friend mentioning that one of her kids thought I was strict. So, I thought I would get my kids' opinions. When I asked them if they thought I was strict, they laughed and said, no! This was great to hear because when I was a teenager, I can remember a ton of my friends rebelling because they had strict parents. So, my was not to be strict. Strict can be defined as parents who talk at their kids rather than with them. They are more concerned about having kids obey then having their kids take ownership of why they are obeying. Strict parents don't allow their kids to express themselves deeply enough. So, before I ever heard the Lord speak to me about my calling to be a Mother of Change, I was already taking steps to create change in my home by encouraging my kids to grow alongside me. When my girls were between the ages of seven and eleven, I consecrated my life to Yahweh like no other time in my life, and I did it for my kids. I mentioned earlier that I fasted from Christian music that had any secular flavor. I died to the flesh. I didn't want my kids having any taste for the things of the world. So, for that season, I raised them with hymns and classical music. It was a season in life that I encouraged my girls to learn how to become domestic because I felt it was a lost art in our culture. Girls aren't taught how to take care of the household these days.

# Mama, raise your daughter

# to honor Yahweh.

I wanted my daughters to be equipped to run a home for the glory of God. I wanted them to learn some old-school skills, and they were all in. They surpassed me years ago in their abilities to live sustainably. Between the two of them, they have some fabulous skills and enjoy learning new ones.

I believe providing our daughters the opportunity to learn domestic skills is a gift to their future families and humanity. I know that we have benefited from all that my daughters know how to do. Some of their homestead abilities include: making candles, soap, bread, cheese, yogurt, daughter butchering live chickens, and crochet.

(Photo: My twenty-one-year-old daughter)

Remember, I said I wanted to raise maidens of virtue, and I define that as women who love and serve God with reverence.

---

*Who can find a virtuous woman? for her price is far above rubies.*

*The heart of her husband doth safely trust in her, so that he shall have no need of spoil.*

*She will do him good and not evil all the days of her life.*

*She seeketh wool, and flax, and worketh willingly with her hands.*

*She is like the merchants' ships; she bringeth her food from afar.*

*She riseth also while it is yet night, and giveth meat to her household, and a portion to her maidens.*

*She considereth a field, and buyeth it: with the fruit of her hands she planteth a vineyard.*

*She girdeth her loins with strength, and strengtheneth her arms.*

*She perceiveth that her merchandise is good: her candle goeth not out by night.*

*She layeth her hands to the spindle, and her hands hold the distaff.*

---

*She stretcheth out her hand to the poor; yea, she reacheth forth her hands to the needy.*

*She is not afraid of the snow for her household: for all her household are clothed with scarlet.*

*She maketh herself coverings of tapestry; her clothing is silk and purple.*

*Her husband is known in the gates, when he sitteth among the elders of the land.*

*She maketh fine linen, and selleth it; and delivereth girdles unto the merchant.*

*Strength and honour are her clothing; and she shall rejoice in time to come.*

*She openeth her mouth with wisdom; and in her tongue is the law of kindness.*

*She looketh well to the ways of her household, and eateth not the bread of idleness.*

*Her children arise up, and call her blessed; her husband also, and he praiseth her.*

*Many daughters have done virtuously, but thou excellest them all.*

*Favour is deceitful, and beauty is vain: but a woman that feareth the LORD, she shall be praised.*

*Give her of the fruit of her hands; and let her own works praise her in the gates.*

*(Prov. 31:10-31)*

---

Proverbs 31 provides a framework not only for us but for raising our daughters as well. This chapter is Yahweh's blueprint for His daughters, so we should adopt it as a standard for our daughters.

## LESSONS FROM PROVERBS 31

Who is the Proverbs 31 woman?

She is:

1. Wise.
2. Strong.
3. Fearless.
4. Domestic.
5. Generous.
6. Honorable.
7. Industrious.
8. Considerate.
9. An Entrepreneur.

When I look at that list, it makes me realize that the daily effort to be intentional and practicing a death-to-self was worth it! I can look back over my life as a parent to the present time, and I am content with what I see.

Mama, are you parenting with intention? Write down a list of godly desires for your daughters and take the list to the Lord.

I really desired for my girls to be dynamic, grounded, and capable. On top of their domestic skills, I wanted to raise them to be entrepreneurs to give them an opportunity to work from home.

I have been teaching them how to make money from home since they were in elementary school, and now my oldest daughter Bijou is an aspiring filmmaker, and she is a media editor. She has entered film festivals and has done acting on commercials. She also helps to run our family legacy company, McMillion & Co. LLC. Her love is film production, and she has been studying it for seven years. Her goal is to create movies with life-transforming messages, and I know she will do it.

Even though she is a young adult, she has not been interested in dating because she is waiting until the Lord brings the right young man in her life.

Mama, I am sharing this information for the sole purpose of inspiring you to develop your personal narrative for your daughter based upon scripture and prayer.

## Create a narrative for your kids + family.

When God shows you a glimpse of what He has in store for your kid's future, life gets exciting for the entire family, and that's what keeps kids loyal to the family and their calling.

My second daughter, Davae, graduated high school at sixteen and immediately entered college via distance education courses. She is a graphic artist and is due to publish her first book this year. Her dream is to become a motivational speaker, inspiring young women to live as their authentic selves.

*Remember, age is not a limitation for kids to step into their calling.*

The common belief is that kids must wait until they grow up to pursue their calling.

The cultural expectation is for a kid to go to school, graduate, attend college, then in their early to mid-twenties, finally start to pursue their dreams. As I mentioned earlier, I have been raising my kids to pursue their dreams since elementary school. Kids don't have to wait until they are adults to step into their destiny.

The beauty of helping our kids to start early is that we have created a narrative for our family that centers around building a family legacy. We have created platforms for them to work in their unique gifts while working together. My daughters are fulfilled to be at home with their parents because they are encouraged to live out their dreams now, at home.

*Help your kids start doing, not just planning to do.*

I think the feminist movement has shortchanged God's blessings for our daughters. It has diminished the value of being domestic. I can't count the young women I have met that can't cook or clean properly. It's no wonder families are a wreck when a woman doesn't find value in her God-ordained position to nurture and create a tapestry of beauty in her home.

The lie that satan is putting it out is that women can't be successful and domestic or modest and attractive at the same time. It's an either-or mentality that is limiting, which leaves women to choose one or the other. It's small thinking and very limited.

---

*Domestic: relating to the running of a home or to family relations. (Google Dictionary)*

---

I believe it's possible to be both feminine and strong. I never wanted to limit my daughters by making them fit into average stereotypes, especially the teen girl one! I wanted them to identify themselves as being daughters of God above anything else.

We focused on growing their confidence based on their relationship with God. I remember being in high school and looking for love in all the wrong places. Nothing about the experience was a happy place for me. Even while I was in school, it felt like a shallow experience filled with cliques, fake people, and teens driven by hormones and drama. There was nothing within me that wanted to put my girls in that kind of environment. I wanted to help mold and shape them by allowing them to form their personal value without peer pressure to live counter who Christ, who was calling them to be. Our daughters should feel wanted and needed in our homes.

*They should feel valued + cherished.*

I know some daughters are being taught to take care of a home, but they suffer from bitterness.

If this is your case I would suggest:

1. Re-evaluating if they are having enough balan ce in their workload. If I see my girls showing signs of burnout. I make sure to take time to look for ways to fill their *love tank,* plus I change up their duties. There are five love languages, and it's essential to show your kids appreciation via their love language. See #3 for more on this topic.

2. If everyone in the family is doing their fair share and your daughter still has a bad attitude, I would suspect there is a lack of gratitude. If there is a lack of gratitude that must be dealt with to gain her heart. See the chapter that deals with ungratefulness.

3. Show appreciation for your kid's hard work. Our kids work harder than most kids I know. They have a lot of responsibilities. So, we have a vacation fund that we contribute to, no matter what our financial status was over the years. Then once a year, we take the kids on vacation for

all their dedication. When we start getting burned out from our schedule, it's nice to have something to look forward to for all of us mentally.

I raised the girls to enjoy being domestic by giving them the fruit of their hands. Because they were both grateful, they were content to create and make things for the whole family to enjoy and use. We did have our moments with some episodes, but I used deductive reasoning and a lot of prayer with the power of effective communication to win them over each time.

I desired to raise them to be intelligent, confident, capable, and positioned to do great things in the kingdom of God. I even told Davae to start writing a book on becoming a teen millionaire when she was thirteen. I encouraged her to start the book even though she didn't finish it because I wanted her to know that I believe that she could achieve it. More importantly, I wanted her to think that she could do it. She reminds me that she still has time to make that benchmark. While most teens are worried about texts, boyfriends, school sports, and shopping, my girls are building our family brand and growing mad skills in business and in their calling.

Part of my strategy to raise confident young women was to raise them to understand their value was not measured by their appearance or body shape. Instead, worth comes from our inheritance in Yahweh, our creator.

He has created us into His masterpiece! So personal identity and self-respect were at the forefront of raising *daughters of change.*

212

To create that mix meant, I had to instill strong values in them and show them the importance of modesty. I think a lot of parents who adopt modesty make some big mistakes in their focus.

## WRONG MODESTY FOCUS:

1. Clothes.
2. Men's perception.
3. Religion.

Making clothes the focus of modesty is putting an over-emphasis on the dos and don'ts of a wardrobe. Families become legalistic about clothes, and I think it's a disservice towards cultivating a heart of modesty.

Then there is a strong belief that women shouldn't dress to entice men. While I agree that we shouldn't, I think it's also the wrong emphasis because girls can easily become irritated with men because they can't wear certain clothes because "men have issues with lust." I have seen that play a lot of times in families. Girls who are raised with this as the primary focus tend to forsake modesty while developing an irritation with men for making them have to limit their clothes because of their lust issues.

Then there is the religious modesty angle, and I can say this focal point breeds all kinds of evil, including legalism, salvation by works, criticalness, and judgementalism. It comes with a lot of rules and dos and don'ts. I also don't see a lot of depth to girls who are raised with religion as the purpose of their clothing choice. Strict comes to mind for this mindset.

So what should be the focal point? Let me share a modesty strategy that works! But before we dive into it, let me tell you why modesty is important to teach your daughters.

# THREE REASONS TO ADOPT MODESTY

1. It honors God.
a. What? know ye not that your body is the temple of the Holy Ghost *which is* in you, which ye have of God, and ye are not your own? (1 Cor. 6:19)
b. In like manner also, that women adorn themselves in modest apparel (1 Tim. 2:9)
2. It honors self.
a. Strength and honor are her clothing (Prov. 31:25)
3. It shows others your personal confidence.

Remember, satan has an agenda, as I mentioned earlier. When it comes to clothing, he has two strategies to get girls and women to live counter to the Bible.

## SATAN'S GAMEPLAN

**Strategy 1:** Have women dress like men, and create gender-neutral clothes, decreasing feminity.

- The woman shall **not wear** that which pertaineth unto a **man**, neither shall a man put on a woman's garment: for all that do so are abomination unto the LORD thy God. (Deut. 22:5)

**Strategy 2:** Sexualize women and even children by showing nakedness.

- I counsel you to buy from me gold refined by fire, so that you may be rich, and white garments so that you may clothe yourself and the **shame of your nakedness** may not be seen, (Rev. 3:18)

- Thus says the Lord GOD, Because your lust was poured out and your **nakedness uncovered** in your whorings with your lovers... (Ez. 16:35)

When I was growing up, I was never taught about modesty, and I used to show my body. I couldn't imagine leaving the house without my hoop earrings and cleavage. They went hand in hand. So modesty for me has been a journey for sure. After I got married and moved to Greece, I had my first big wake up call. Just before I met my husband, I recommitted my life to Christ at twenty-two-years old.

Almost immediately, I started to cover up my body. Well, at least it felt like it was compared to my pre-commitment wardrobe. However, one day after a church service, I had a church member pull me aside to let me know that the Greek churchgoers felt that my clothes were too showy for church clothes. To be honest, I remember being bothered because compared to my wardrobe a year before, I thought I was pretty covered. I guess I must not have listened because sometime later I had a friend come over to visit my house and I could tell she wanted to share something with me, but she was having trouble getting it out. Finally, she told me that it was my clothes and that they were too immodest for church. Okay, Lord, okay. At that point, I realized the problem must be me and not others. So, I decided to listen finally, and I ordered some new clothes.

The interesting thing is that when I look back at that season of my life, I feel my clothes looked extremely masculine. I started to wear docker type of women pants with a button-up long sleeve shirts from a popular catalog store. Do you see what happened? I went from satan's second strategy to his first one! I can see it so clearly in retrospect.

Anyhow, after I came back to the states, I started to slip from my standard because I never got the heart of modesty. It became religion for me, and yes, I began to manifest that evil fruit I mentioned earlier about becoming legalistic.

So Yahweh had to teach me that salvation is not gained by works or by how we dress. Unfortunately, I took this information wrong, and I thought this meant God didn't care what we wore, and what do you know? I slipped back into dressing in tight jeans, low cut tank tops, and my stomach showing! It truly is a slippery slope. But, the Lord started to convict my heart, and I took my conviction to my husband, and he brushed it off and said, "hun, guys would look at you if you were wearing a potato sack." Do you see what happened? We made modesty about a man's perception, which was #2 of a wrong modesty focus.

Some time went by, and one day, while we were in a prayer room, my husband tapped me on the shoulder and said, "hun, you can't wear those tight jeans anymore." Apparently, the Lord convicted him because he was the one that bought them for me. Here we were trying to minister to teens about personal value, and he said my clothes selection was sending a mixed message. Ouch! He was right; I was back to looking from affirmation from society, showing off my body.

Finally, I was starting to understand that modesty was about so much more than clothes. It was about heart change. It was about a lifestyle change.

Then something fabulous happened. My husband, who rarely shops for clothes, came home with a bag of gorgeous skirts. They had a bohemian flare and looked great on me.

At first, I mostly just wore them to church, but then I felt like I wasn't consistent. I didn't want to be a "Sunday Christian." I wanted to be fully me all the time. I figured if I wore skirts to church to be modest, then why wasn't wearing them all the time? Something beautiful started to happen. I made a shift in my mind and heart, and getting dressed was no longer about do's and don'ts. It wasn't about enticing or not enticing men. It was about honoring God and understanding my value in Him. It became about embracing my feminity. I started to cover my body whether or not I was around other men because it wasn't about men. It was about personal dignity and a desire to take the Word at face value. There was no more "who cares what you wear because men will still look at you" because men were devoid of my mind when thinking about my clothes selection. I started to wear modest clothes all day every day, not because I felt like a slave but because I felt free! My value was no longer based upon my body that was being promoted like a package. I admit I went through a stage where I was skirt obsessed. I was always buying them. I seriously love skirts. I feel no limitations being modest; I wear clothes that I love to live in and so do my daughters. Our clothes rule is if we don't love something, we don't get it.

During my enlightenment, I decided to share my excitement with the girls. It was about seven years ago when I mentioned to them, "what if we wear skirts all the time? What if wasn't just church clothes? What if we were the same all the time?" I let them explore the idea with me. They weren't sure what to think about it, but after their daddy started noticing them and giving them compliments, they became enamored with feminity too.

I see now that the Lord was preparing us because satan would be entering into the clothing industry to try to take over the market with gender-confused clothing. I believe that the Lord is releas-ing this message for such a time as this so that you can confidently and unashamedly grasp onto Biblical feminity and stand opposed to the enemy's plan.

In raising my girls, this is the strategy that I used to capture their hearts.

### A MODESTY STRATEGY

1. Focus on personal worth.
2. Leave men out of the equation.
3. Dress unto the Lord.

Our clothing is an outward expression of our personal value. We dress with intention because we respect ourselves. I will even mention that my oldest daughter has a stronger modesty stand-ard than I do. Even at twenty, she doesn't feel comfortable showing her arms. She may change her mind later, but that is her conviction. I do wear sleeveless tops, but I respect her desire to honor God with her clothing choices.

I realize there are going to be families who have a higher modesty standard than us, and I completely admire that. I always encourage family's not to base their standards on other people's ideas. We can definitely learn from others, but we have to make sure to ask God what His leading is for our family in every area. This helps us not to become overly religious in our clothing choices.

The bottom line is I want my girls to be respected and honored because of the personage and who they are as contributors to society. I don't want them to define their self-worth by how many men look at them. After all, I remind them about how many young men have porn problems, and those are the same men who will most likely cheat on their wives and kids. I want them to want more for their lives. I want them to trust God to supply for their every need according to His riches and glory so that they don't look for love in all the wrong places.

Teach your daughters that dressing modestly is their dialog with society that says they are confident in who they are.

Encourage your girls to challenge culture. My girls love to let people know they don't have to show thighs or cleavage, to validate themselves.

My girls and I leave men out of the equation when forming our clothing standard. We don't base what we wear with men in mind. In other words, we don't say, "Will this stumble a man?" Our modesty is deeper than that. True, we don't want to stumble any believer, man or woman with any part of our life. But when it comes to our wardrobe, we dress to magnify God. We ask questions like, will I deter from being light if I wear this? Our modesty is consistent around men or not. My girls and I don't get dressed in front of each other because we have modesty standards even with each other. This is a long way from where I came from when I was younger. During all of this growth, I have kept open dialog and communication with the girls. This is what separates this parenting style from strict parenting. Getting your girl's heart should always be your top priority because you want them to have ownership and form their own convictions. It's about communication.

My girls each have their own unique style, and I encourage them to have fun with their wardrobe. It is always such a blessing to me when people stop my girls at the store to compliment them on their outfits. In those moments, I point out how neat it is that they don't have to show their merchandise to be noticed. People are drawn to their inner light. I think it's great that they know how to stay modest and regal.

Clothing is important to God. He does want His daughters to be respected and treated with decency.

Think about how many marriages end in divorce because lust was at the forefront of the relationship. We don't do our girls any favors if we allow them to show their bodies.

I know some girls dress sexy and say they do it for self and those girls have a big issue with self-denial. They have bought into a satanic mindset. It's destructive and telling.

So, mama, I encourage you to take the idea of living modestly to the Lord for yourself and your daughters.

Dressing modestly is an
act of obedience and
love for Yahweh, and love of self.

—EmmaSara

# Take Action

Three reasons to adopt modesty:

_____

_____

_____

Three wrong modesty focuses:

_____

_____

_____

How are you being an example of modesty to your daughter?

_____

_____

Three modesty strategies that work:

_____

_____

_____

_____

*Dressing modestly*

*reveals dignity.*

*— Emma Sara*

# Overstepping Boundaries

I had a situation this week where one of the kids did something that they aren't allowed to do. They were given a little leeway to do a project, and without wasting any time, they used the opportunity to go beyond the boundary that was previously set up for them. Past experiences have proven to me that if a kid has purposely gone beyond a set boundary, they will end up breaking each of the four non-negotiables mentioned in this book. The first one they will break is lacking gratefulness. If you increase your kid's boundary area and they go past it, it reveals ungratefulness for the extra trust they were just given. If they make an excuse for why they went past it, they then enter into manipulation and lying because they know good and well they stepped into no man's land—a place they should never venture!

The moment they start lying or manipulating, they are showing further signs of disrespect! If they do both, watch out! This is the highest degree of offense in my book. As a result of rebellion, they have broken all four of the non-negotiables! Getting back to my situation, not only did I immediately revoke the extra boundary space extended, but I also set a new boundary beyond what was previously had!

When dealing with such an offense as broken trust, it's essential to act quickly. If you have constant situations where one of your kids tends to "forget" the boundary rules, my friend suggested creating a boundary contract that your child signs. Then there would be less room for excuses about a lack of clarity or understanding. Since relational work must be done to regain privileges, this could be a useful tool. Clear communication can be increased when there are written terms. Whatever you decide to do, make sure boundary markers are established and monitored. Keeping kids accountable is the bottom line. Overstepping a boundary sets off a siren to let you know that your kid is having a heart issue, even if just for a moment. So make sure to cover them with prayer and positive affirmations.

**Affirmations for your child:**

_____ respects God-given authority.

_____ tells the truth.

_____ does not use manipulation.

_____ has an attitude of gratitude.

# *Prayer*

Father, thank you that _____ is submitted to you. Lord, please help _____ desire to serve you in spirit and truth. Help my son/daughter not to love the world because your love is within him/her, and light has no part with darkness. Father help my child to hate lying and to be a truth-teller. In your name Yeshua, amen.

*Keeping kids accountable*

*is the bottom line.*

*-EmmaSara*

# Chapter 6

## World Changer Mom

6.1 Mom Chat
6.2 Lions and Tigers, Oh My!
6.3 A Multi-Generational Mindset
6.4 C.H.A.N.G.E

# Mom Chat

I believe the strength of our nation rests upon the shoulders of moms like you to bring change to our country. You can bring change by teaching godly standards to your children and, most importantly, by living them out. With that said, mama, can I ask you to do something? You have made it to this point. You have come too far to turn back now! You are about to take a deep dive into cultural issues, and instead of positioning yourself according to political views, can I ask you to please leave your political hat at the door?

Can I ask you to focus on being God motivated, rather than politically motivated?

We are about to visit some topics that can be challenging to tackle, except by the grace of God. Please understand that it's not my heart to cast judgment or be legalistic on such relevant topics. Some things are going on in the nation that requires us to press into God. I realize some readers may feel a little on defense, but I don't mean to push. I am aiming to inspire you to dig deeper into the pursuit of Godly truth. So, pray and ask the Lord how to respond to this section. Ask Jesus to reveal profound truths that can only be uncovered by the Holy Spirit, according to Jeremiah 33:3. Also, ask God to calibrate your heart and then read on.

# Prayer

Father, search me, know me. Uncover areas in my heart that I need to surrender to you. Calibrate my heart, Lord. Line it up with your best for my household. Help me to be a mother that will be known for creating change in my community for your glory! In Jesus name, amen.

# Lions and Tigers, Oh My!

We expect that our kids will learn about the alphabet and animals in school, but sex-education for five-year-olds? Just the thought should give us a cause for concern, let alone the fact that this is already going on in many schools!

Remember, the Father takes delight when moms protect their children by being aware of the schemes of the enemy. So, this topic is about awareness. Mama, this is a call to action! I didn't write this book to put down people's lifestyle choices. Nor did I write this book to tell adults how to interact with one another. If you have a personal political stance, I am not even trying to tell you what to do in that area because I am not politically motivated, I am God motivated as I mentioned before. I am more concerned about what God would have me do than what my indulgent heart would have me do. I vote morality, period. I know you may be thinking, "Is that even possible?" I will say this, ask Yahweh each to guide you each time you vote. Let the Spirit lead you.

We have standards for voting, and I am happy to share my shortlist with you.

Unfortunately, we shouldn't solely base our vote upon a candidate's personal behavior because it seems they all have issues if we dig deep enough. I wonder how many people would vote for King David from the Bible if he ran in our next election. He was a murderer and adulterer, yet he was the Lord's anointed and described as having a heart that was after Yahweh. Even with all his sinful ways, he established God's law over the people, and he sought to serve Yahweh and Yahweh alone. The main point is that David was an upholder of God's government at the end of the day. So in all things, let us seek God for His guidance.

Mama, I am blowing the horn for our nation to wake up! Isaiah 58 says to blow the shofar and tell My people of their transgressions or sins! This means the people of God have to be reminded about how far they have strayed from Yahweh as a nation! There is nothing new under the sun (Eccl. 1:9).

Satan is alive and moving in our nation and around the world! He is a liar and a manipulator! He is a seducer and only knows how to operate counter to Yahweh.

My kids know their mama is a woman of resolve who subdues her flesh. I do it because I realize satan wants me to give in to worldly desires and to be lackadaisical. I also know he wants to destroy our families by introducing hurt, rage, and pain in our homes! So I will not be his sucker! I will not be his puppet!

I was raised in East Los Angeles on the violent side of town when I was small, so I know what it means to be a sucker, and this woman is not one!

I will not dance on a string while satan makes me move to his circus tune.

I'm reminded time and time again, "My way or Yahweh?" Unless you have personally chosen to put on the mind of Christ in every situation and every circumstance, you can quickly become like a puppet on a string dancing like a fool to the tune of the enemy. Do you want to be like a puppet on a string, or do you want to put on the mind of Christ concerning all things? Also, Mama, here's a question, "Are you raising sons, daughters, or hens?" What? Hens? No, I am not talking about female chickens! I am talking about another term used to identify children! I don't know about you, but I am not raising "hens." I am raising entirely male and fully female children, and I hope you are too.

"Hen" is the new gender-neutral term for either a male or female who is not associating with their true nature!

For it is written,

---

"that at the beginning, the Creator 'made them male and female'" (Matt. 19:4 NIV).

---

I am a Warrior Queen, but I am not a hater! My hope is that people from all walks of life would believe in Yeshua/Jesus and be saved. I have friends and family that are practicing lifestyles that I don't agree with, but I don't love them any less for their choices. I don't believe in shoving my belief system down anyone's throat. However, I also feel it's unloving not to present truth according to the

Word if the Spirit leads me. Yes, I said, "If I'm led." Not everyone is ready to hear the truth, according to the Bible. However, I have compassion for all walks of life because I was personally living lawlessly and without morals for a long season in my life. I think of all the people that were kind to me despite my lifestyle choices, and for that, I am grateful. Ultimately, each individual must stand in front of God for their life choices. We shouldn't beat people with the Word, and I get that. I know some people can get very angry when certain topics come up. However, I want my hands to be clean concerning this topic. I want it to be understood that I am not writing from a place of anger or even religion. Instead, my intent is to protect the innocence of children.

Therefore, I write to you because you are a guardian of your children, and I am calling you out to protect them out of a heart of love. I didn't want to have kids because I thought the world was too evil, but God changed my heart and told me He would equip me to protect them. Not only has He allowed me to protect my children, but also other children, by providing education to moms who have been subject to a delusion by satan himself. I am passionate about educating moms about protecting their children from the violations of the enemy. Mama, remember kids molest kids too. Studies show that children who are exposed to early sexuality are those who are prone to become abusers.

---

*Researchers have found that child sexual abusers exhibited heightened sexuality in childhood.*[1]

---

Who do you think causes kids to get molested? Who do you think wants to sexualize our kids? Satan. Who do you think wants you to let down your guard? Who do you think wants to put transgender sex education in your preschooler's head? Satan! How do I know that? Because God created them male and female, and satan is a liar, so he will cause confusion about gender!

---

For God is not the author of confusion but of peace. (1 Cor. 14:33)

---

The acts of Transvestism or people dressing up as the opposite sex is not new—it has been a part of pagan worship for centuries. One gender-neutral children's clothing line looks more like a Satanist cult clothing line than it does a kid's line. Yet, Hollywood parents are buying it up. One advertisement had a kid with a Baphomet goat head mask. Baphomet is an occult figure and deity. To top it off, the kid models look angry and disturbed.

If you want to see the spirit behind this blurred gender movement, do a web search for "divine androgyne." The search will quickly reveal the spirit behind the agenda. However, pray first for guidance and make sure your kids are not around because it is R-rated and demonic. If you're visual and hold images in your mind, then by-pass the search. Just know that it is the real deal. Another telling search is "transvestite kids." It shows the strong push to sexualize kids. Even if a kid is straight or feeling confused about their gender, a mother should protect her child from being sexualized at any stage of adolescence! Instead, kids are being served up daily on the altar of satan and all his demonic perversion! In biblical days, open paganism was rampant, so God in His wisdom gave laws to His children to keep them from adopting godless ways. Remember, gender-neutral clothes are marketed with a satanic purpose, so don't be fooled. Satan loves to oppose God's ways, and he loves families to go along with him.

---

Therefore it was written, "A woman must not wear men's clothing, nor a man wear women's clothing, for the LORD your God detests anyone who does this." (Duet . 22:5)

---

Mama be AWARE! Don't let the enemy fool you. Know your adversary. Know his schemes. Get some strategy and show the enemy he has messed with the wrong woman!

Sweden is said to be one of the most atheistic countries in the world and they are starting kids as early as preschool without gender specifications.[16] As a matter of fact, I read that they are working hard to blur the lines for kids! Two Swedish preschools are noted as going to great lengths to de-emphasize gender and are encouraging kids to challenge and CROSS gender boundaries![17]

This isn't just going on abroad!

California is known as a progressive state, and they are creating guidelines to indoctrinate kids with the trans-gender lifestyle by providing books like My Princess Boy by

Cheryl Kilodavis, written for small children. Previous state guidelines say,

---

"It is an age-appropriate book that can be used to demonstrate gender differences and inclusion." 12

*Under "Parenting with the Community" under Section 1189, (April 2019 -California) it states, "Members of the community who defy traditional stereotypes (e.g., women firefighters, male nurses, and stay-at-home fathers/guardians/caretakers) could be invited as guest speakers to share about their jobs and to serve as role models and myth busters. Be sure to include individuals of all genders, including people who are transgender."*[18]

---

I understand that people have different lifestyles. However, don't kids deal with enough confusion as they are growing up? I looked over the My Princess Boy book and read some comment reviews, and here are some that speak for themselves!

---

➢ *Princess Boy sounds like a narcissist obsessed with himself. Not healthy at all. —Dr. C*
➢ *If a "princess boy" exists, it's because the parents allowed and/or advocated it. Not on my watch. Ever. My boy will be indoctrinated as a conventional boy and if later in life. If he comes out as gay, that's cool. But I'm not facilitating it. Not one bit. —a Dad*
➢ *I think princess boy needs to be helped out of his confusion. Before he thinks wearing girl clothes and*

*cutting off his healthy body parts are what make people truly happy in life. Happiness is not found trying to impersonate the opposite sex—princess boy has to accept who he is and ask himself why he wants to be somebody else—what happened that made him so uncomfortable being in his own skin.*

---

It's hard not to agree with some of these comments once you read the book. It's clear this book will cause greater problems rather than create solutions for small children!

My greatest concern comes from understanding that children go through a myriad of feelings, including self-rejection, fear, insecurity, and a ton of other common adolescent emotions. As a parent, I have made it my goal to teach my kids how much value they give to this earth simply by being alive!

I consider them highly capable, intelligent, a pleasure to be around, and still, they have each had moments of insecurity, self-doubt, and even self-rejection without inviting external factors like gender confusion to add to the mix.

Why add another area for potential insecurity and confusion in a kid's life? I can only imagine the level of confusion a boy must go through when he is told he doesn't have to be a female or male, only to realize at some point that his body parts don't align with his gender decision to "be a female." The boy who chooses to live as a girl might say, "Mama, I am a girl, right? This means I will be able to have kids just like you, right?" Logically, that would be the hope of a little girl who desires to be a mom one day. What then? Why would anyone want to add more despair to a child's life by setting them up to feel incompetent about what their body cannot do?

Yet the enemy is force-feeding our children at every level and getting away with it! They even have Drag Queen Story Hours in libraries. To make matters worse, a particular storytime drag queen was listed as a lifetime sex offender as of October 2019.[2]

Remember that public libraries are funded by the public, which means you. Why sit back and take this? The bigger this movement gets, the more powerful it is to seduce our children. Where are the parents to speak up and protect their children? What happened to battling for our kids? Where are the mama bears? Children's mental health is of utmost importance, and that's why satan wants to bring such confusion to our children!

Rebuke the spirit of confusion in Jesus's name!

If you have been silent, Mama ask the Lord to remove any blinders in your life quickly! Ask Him to empower you to do impacting things for the protection of your children.

As a mama, my goal is to raise sons who have a strong self-identity. However, because of ignorance and believing the world's lie, I was buying into feminizing my first son without realizing it! Thank the Lord God Almighty that He gave me eyes to see how I was inflicting potential damage on him early on, so we were able to do an about-face! Let me make it clear; my focus in writing is not to deal with adult lifestyle choices. Instead, the focus is on adults who are trying to indoctrinate our kids to accept their lifestyle choices. The aim is to point out how school systems are purposely trying to confuse our children by planting "options" for gender choice in their curriculum.

According to the CDC:

---

*Suicide is a leading cause of death in the US. Suicide rates increased in nearly every state from 1999 through 2016. Mental health conditions are often seen as the cause of suicide.[3]*

---

I am concerned that the curriculum will harm society's children because it is sowing confusion into children that can lead to depression and, in some severe cases, could lead to suicide.  This issue must be met with prayer and parental action! Mama, do not stay silent when your children are being taught principles that go against your convictions. Schools should be focused on academics and not indoctrination to sexual promiscuity! Be proactive to help you schools be a safer place for kids.

# Take Action

Who wants to sexualize children?

_____

How were you challenged by the topics discussed in this chapter?

_____

_____

_____

Ask God how you can be more vigilant to protect your kids and list two ways:

_____

_____

_____

Have you been blinded about safety issues? Repent. Yahweh is good to forgive and empower. List areas that need attention in your home:

_____

_____

_____

Show the enemy he has

messed with the wrong woman!

– EmmaSara

# A Multi-Generational Mindset

Since we live in a microwave, instant gratification culture, the awareness of generational legacy seems to be diminishing. I find that people have no problem thinking about long-term environmental impact, but they are negating the critical focus of generational impact. I think about countries that have a diminishing population count because repopulation is down. Why some nations would purposely choose to put a halt to the repopulation of their country's citizens is mind-boggling to me! When I did a quick search for the word "generation" in a Bible app, it appeared over two hundred times! I think it's safe to assume that legacy and generational focus are important to God. So if it is essential to God that a righteous generation fills the earth, then it is crucial to the enemy to try to extinguish it! This is currently happening through genocide, population control, and convincing people that children are a burden rather than a blessing! It's time to take back ground in this area! If you have been under the delusion of the enemy in this area in the smallest way, you need to repent! As a people of God, we can't partner with satan and his plan to wipe out God's creation!

> *"Do not give any of your children to be sacrificed to Molek, for you must not profane the name of your God. I am the LORD." (Lev. 18:21 NIV)*

I realize this is a touchy subject in our nation right now, but I come to you as a daughter of the Most High on the topic! Just last month, I watched a video of an abortion doctor showing parts of a baby's dismembered fingers, and he had a smile on his face! He was so pleased as he explained that this woman could now go on and pursue her goals of finishing college without having to worry about a baby! Since when did pursuing your goals become grounds to end life?

That video brought up a memory for me. I will never forget my twelve-week sonogram with my first pregnancy. I was fascinated and excited to see my baby girl sucking her thumb so early on! I came to work the next day to share the news with my manager, and I can remember telling him, "I just don't understand how people can risk their lives to save the trees, but those same people are fighting to kill babies in utero!" He turned and looked at me with a quiet, pondering look. He just paused and didn't know what to say. He just mumbled, "I don't know." Later that year, I found out that his wife aborted their baby at some point in their marriage because she didn't want kids. I felt so sad for him. I felt sad for her.

Now we have gotten to a point in society where sacrificing kids on the altar of career and personal freedom has become commonplace. I know some reading this will cry out for the rights of the mother and the safety of a woman. However, I believe it's never okay to perform a late-term abortion. How can I make such a strong statement? I watched an interview with a medical doctor who gave his professional insight that there is never a reason to perform a late-term abortion to save a mother. He said that if the mother were in a position of life or death, they would deliver the baby early to save the mom. So, why would any woman cheer for a late-term pregnancy death sentence? This year I was disturbed to watch as a bill passed in a state to perform late-term abortions, and a bunch of women stood to cheer this bill passing!

My God!

My God!

My heart was grieved within me that we have come to a time when the same women who are supposed to nurture and care for children would applaud the murder of babies in the third trimester of gestation!

When a woman can applaud such an act, the nation should shudder and hide because Yahweh is on the throne, and the blood of those babies will cry out! Oh Lord, spare this nation! Why mention this topic in a parenting book? Because this is not just any parenting book, this is a call to Mothers of CHANGE around the world to rise up and stand with Yahweh and HIS PRECEPTS to raise up a generation that fears Him and honors His word in spirit and truth.

You don't have to agree with me on this topic, but if you call yourself a believer, make sure to check out how Yahweh feels about infant sacrifice. Pray for discernment on the subject.

A legacy continues in life, bad or good. What kind of legacy mindset are you sowing into your children?

If you are a Mother of Change, you have a generational focus. You consider your present and future grandchildren and great-great-grandchildren!

- I believe you are here because you are hungry for change, and Yahweh is ready to equip you as a Mother of Change.

- I believe that you want to follow God's word and His ways.

- I believe that you want to repent for partnering with the enemy in any way, shape, or form!

- I believe that you are not afraid to stand upon the written Word of God.

- I believe that you love righteousness more than pleasure.

- I believe that you want to glorify Yahweh in all that you say and do, especially when it comes to raising your kids to be world changers!

How will your kids change the world? The most significant change they can bring is to be a light to this world that has grown so dim because the Spirit says, "ENOUGH! ENOUGH! ENOUGH!"

*I believe you are the generation of them that seek him, that seek thy face...*
  *(Psalms 24:6)*

I believe God is raising up a generation of mothers who will rise to their high calling to raise up a holy generation who will take back what the enemy has stolen from our nation and world!

I believe you are a Mother of Change!

I believe you are a Warrior Queen!

It's time, Mama! This is the hour to redeem the time!

It's time to impact the world for the better with the fruit of your womb and/or the children of your heart by teaching them God's ways!

As believers, we all have an assigned territory.

Will you proclaim that your generation and generation to come will sit on the throne of the territory Yahweh has assigned to you? Will you reach out to God and ask Him to change your home atmosphere and dynamics radically?

If everything within you is screaming, "Yes!" then make your proclamation out loud so all the angels can rejoice that a Mother of Change has just been armed for battle. It's time to take back all the territory that the enemy has encroached upon for the last time!

## Rise up Mother of Change!

Rise up!

You are equipped to protect your children.

You are ready for the battle!

*You are a Mother of Change!*

# C.H.A.N.G.E

Mama, you did it! Upon completing this chapter, **you graduated from the first phase of the Mother of Change training!** To help you execute becoming a Mother of Change, I created this easy to remember six-point system to keep you focused and on track.

You should now have enough information and training under your belt to execute C.H.A.N.G.E

This system will allow you to protect your kids by putting what you learned into action quickly. When you find yourself falling back into old patterns, remind yourself, I need to C.H.A.N.G.E.

Remember, be intentional to practice the **C.H.A.N.G.E.** to create a positive change in your parenting style and, most importantly, to safeguard your kids.

Here is what each letter stands for:

**C**-onscious. **H**-ear. **A**-ware. **N**-otice. **G**-ear-up. **E**-ngage.

<u>C</u>onscious of the enemy's plans. This means we need to be *mindful* of the opposition. He comes to kill and steal and destroy the family. So, it's pivotal that we stay a step ahead of his schemes to entice and/or cause injury to our kids. Chapter three contains your strategy to stay *mindful*.

Scripture says we are to be as wise as serpents. We can do that by understanding how satan operates to bring destruction to families and especially to kids.

Hear the Voice of the Lord. So many times, we can get busy with family life that we fail to make time to press into God. We get bombarded with life, and quiet time in prayer can become a luxury. Mama, please make time to hear from your creator and heavenly dad. He wants to speak to you and give you instructions for your family. He wants you to bring all your decisions to Him, big or small.

I can remember one time I was listening to an audio message of an older woman encouraging a young mom that she didn't have to worry about not reading the Word or having alone time with God because it wasn't her "season." I understand as moms; we have more times than others to dig into the Word. However, I can remember being in my mid-twenties and feeling like that was foolish advice because it was giving this mom a license not to carve out time with God. I remember wishing she told her not to be hard on herself but to find times to fill up spiritually. God should be at the forefront of our day, even if it's just five minutes. The smaller our kids are, the more we need him. When our kids are small, it can seem like the loneliest days of motherhood, especially if we are stay-at-home moms. When our kids get older, they become ears to talk to, but when they are small, we NEED Jesus to speak to communicate with.

The truth is that I don't think there is any season in life that should feel ok without quiet time with God. We must carve out time to not only pray, but we need to listen also. For me, that time happens in a nice hot bath filled with a mixture of Epsom salts and essential oils. It's just the Spirit and me. It's a time that the world stops, and I can hear clearly. I need that time with God. I desire it.

I look forward to hearing from God and you should to. He is waiting. Will you commit to make time to hear his voice?

Hear the Voice of the Lord. So many times, we can get busy with family life that we fail to make time to press into God. We get bombarded with life, and quiet time in prayer can become a luxury. Mama, please make time to hear from your creator and heavenly dad. He wants to speak to you and give you instructions for your family. He wants you to bring all your decisions to Him, big or small.

One time I was listening to an audio message of an older woman encouraging a young mom that she didn't have to worry about not reading the Word or having alone time with God because it wasn't "her season." I understand as moms; we have more times than others to dig into the Word. However, I can remember being a mom in my mid-twenties and feeling like that was foolish advice because it was giving this mom a license not to carve out time with God. I remember wishing she told her not to be hard on herself but to find times to fill up spiritually. God should be at the forefront of our day, even if it's just five minutes. The smaller our kids are, the more we need him. When our kids are small, it can seem like the loneliest days of motherhood, especially if we are stay-at-home moms. When our kids get older, they become ears to talk to, but when they are small, we NEED Jesus to speak to communicate with.

The truth is that I don't think there is any season in life that should feel ok without quiet time with God. We must carve out time to not only pray, but we need to listen also. For me, that time happens in a nice hot bath filled with a mixture of Epsom salts and essential oils. It's just the Spirit and me. It's a time that the world stops, and I can hear clearly. I need that time with God. I desire it.

I look forward to hearing from God and you should to. He is waiting. Will you commit to make time to hear his voice?

<u>A</u>ware of your surroundings. Be aware! This is such an important point that must not be forgotten. So many kids get victimized or hurt simply because a caregiver was not aware of their surroundings. Chapter seven is a good reminder that you must always be on your guard for your kids because schools are not going to monitor your kids as you will. They will not uphold your standards and personal convictions for your child like you will. Also, be aware of who you allow your kids to play with.

Be aware of who you have babysitting. Remember, sex offenders typically have many victims before they are caught. I know in some cases it can be as high as one hundred! This means background checks are not conclusive. So, be aware and on-guard always. Always listen to your gut feeling if it's sending you a red flag.

<u>N</u>otice your kid's behavior changes. Notice when your kids are showing signs of:

1. Depression.

2. Anxiety.

3. Stress.

4. Crying out for help either silently or violently.

I was watching a video recently online. It was the mom of a school shooter. She caught my attention with this statement, "Everyone always asks me how I didn't notice the signs." I could tell the question was difficult to answer. She mentioned that it was the question that was always pressing her. So, make sure to notice signs that your child is sending out. Notice if there are changes in their behavior or mood. Notice if you need to *Take Action*. If your kid is acting out with ungodly behavior, refer to chapter five, *Dealing with Ungodly Behavior,* to help work through their issues with them.

Gear-Up for the battle. Even soldiers must go to training before going out to battle, and it's no different for us as warrior moms. We must gear up through personal training. Think of this point as the personal development phase. I believe that when a mom's life gets transformed, her whole family can be transformed. So I include my kids in this area of training. You can take them with you to personal development conferences and have them read motivational books. Together listen to inspirational audio messages etc. This focus point is where you become whole: mind, body, and spirit to engage in the battle entirely. Are you ready to gear up?

<u>Engage</u> in the battle. This is the point where you get to create change not only in your home, but you become a force to be reckoned with in your community. Enter the frontlines to stand up for what you believe is right for your kids and your community. I can remember a situation that I engaged in the battle against perversion in my town. My eight kids love books, so we frequent the library quite often. One day I took all the kids to the library, and just after they got settled into the kid's section, I walked by the computer area, which is in the dead center of the library for all to see.

As I walked by, I saw a young man viewing full pornography in the computer section! I reported it to the library staff, and they informed me that since it is a public place, their hands were tied.

What would you have done?

As a Mother of Change, what do you think I did?

You better believe I engaged in the battle!

I went straight to the Sheriff's office, and they confirmed that it was a legal offense. So, finally, the library had an ear to listen to me. Now, a few years later, if you walk into that library, you will find a little sign at every monitor that says viewing inappropriate material is a criminal offense and punishable by a court of law! I felt honored to do a service for my community and the sake of my kid's safety. I engaged in the battle. I spoke up, and I made our library a safer place for children. Will you ask the Lord how you can engage in the battle in your community? Chapter seven can give you a good starting point.

Remember, this six-point framework will help you to...

Execute your duties as a

## Mother of Change.

Be empowered!

Be encouraged!

Now go out and

change the world,

and start at home!

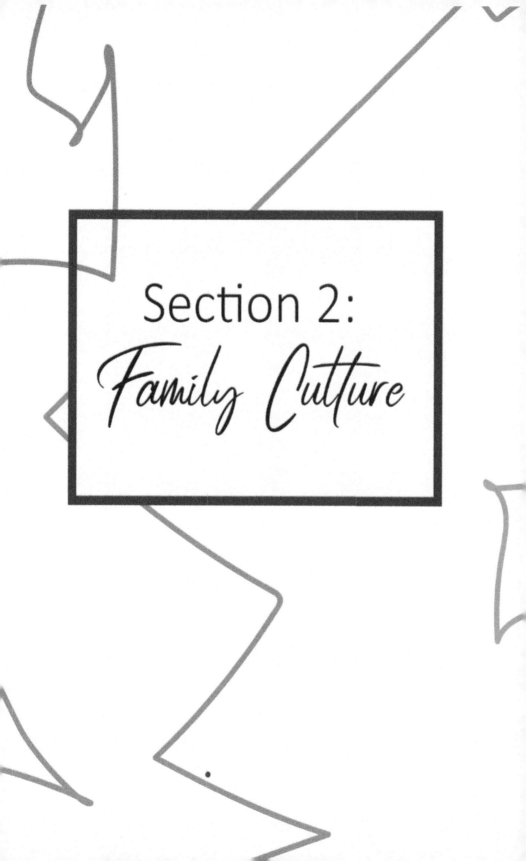

Section 2:
Family Culture

Chapter 7

# Family Legacy

7.1 Family Traditions
7.2 Shabbat
7.3 Communion

# Family Traditions

For thousands of years, traditions have brought communities and families together. There is no better time than the present to re-invent this area in your family's life. So many holidays and traditions have become commercialized that they have lost their power to cultivate beautiful character in your child truly. At some point, I decided to step away from the norm, and I stopped giving my kids gifts for Christmas. Instead, I told the kids that we would have a new focus on being givers rather than receivers for December. Year after year, I would look for ways for our family to be a blessing in our community. My kids caught on quickly and had no problems giving up the practice of getting gifts for Christmas. Eventually we stopped observing Christmas altogether, but we kept the tradition of giving to the needy.

Over the years, we have created traditions of doing beneficial things for humanity like:

- Feeding the homeless.
- Filling shoeboxes to send overseas.
- Filling pillowcase for foster kids stateside.
- This was our community endeavor. We were able to fill a ton of pillowcases with wish-list items for foster kids and it was so gratifying.

Remember, it shouldn't be business as usual for you after you complete this book training. Life should take on a fresh approach. Things should change for the better in your home as you seek to have a Godly home.

Take an inventory of everything your family is involved in and ask yourself:

1. How is this benefiting my child's character?
2. How is it hindering or helping our family and community?

Be open to allow the Lord to show you things so that it will bring about beneficial fruit in your home! As you go through this process, make sure you don't try to justify your current traditions. There are plenty of things we are "allowed to do" as believers and keep our salvation. However, according to 1 Corinthians 10:23, just because something is lawful does not mean it is beneficial! So try to focus on following practices that glorify God.

- Mama, are you willing to edit your life and make decisions for your family that will have a lasting impact on your future generations?
- Count the cost of your lifestyle choices and weigh them out. Make sound choices, and don't cower even at the sound of kids who have become self-absorbed and whimper over God-honoring changes.

Of course, it should be your goal to get them on board with changes and excited about course corrections. I can remember when my kids made the decision not to have a Christmas tree any longer. They decided to do away with it. They studied up on the roots of Christmas, and they got to the point where they didn't want any part of the secularized part of the holiday. Instead of focusing on commercialism, we agreed to make the love of Christ the focus of December and to share His blessing with as many people as we could! As a Mother of Change, you do the world a great big favor when you raise givers instead of takers. Raising contributors is our gift to society!

# Shabbat

Two of our legacy traditions are Shabbat and Family Communion. Shabbat is the biblical term for Sabbath, which is a day of rest. One day in prayer, I heard the Spirit impressing on me that Isaiah 58 was for our family. I didn't tell my husband because I was waiting for confirmation. Days later, my husband didn't go to work, which is rare! When I asked him what was wrong, he said that he was feeling an unsettled stirring in his heart, and he was longing to hear from God. So he went into the backwoods to seek God. Hours later, he came back with a journal entry, and as I leaned over to read his entry, I saw Isaiah 58! This chapter talks about the heart of God to break the bonds of wickedness and the blessing of keeping the seventh-day Sabbath.

---

*Cry aloud, spare not, lift up thy voice like a trumpet, and shew my people their transgression, and the house of Jacob their sins.*

*Yet they seek me daily, and delight to know my ways, as a nation that did righteousness, and forsook not the ordinance of their God: they ask of me the ordinances of justice; they take delight in approaching to God.*

*Wherefore have we fasted, say they, and thou seest not? wherefore have we afflicted our soul, and thou takest no knowledge? Behold, in the day of your fast ye find pleasure, and exact all your labours.*

Behold, ye fast for strife and debate, and to smite with the fist of wickedness: ye shall not fast as ye do this day, to make your voice to be heard on high.

Is it such a fast that I have chosen? a day for a man to afflict his soul? is it to bow down his head as a bulrush, and to spread sackcloth and ashes under him? wilt thou call this a fast, and an acceptable day to the LORD?

Is not this the fast that I have chosen? to loose the bands of wickedness, to undo the heavy burdens, and to let the oppressed go free, and that ye break every yoke?

Is it not to deal thy bread to the hungry, and that thou bring the poor that are cast out to thy house? when thou seest the naked, that thou cover him; and that thou hide not thyself from thine own flesh?

Then shall thy light break forth as the morning, and thine health shall spring forth speedily: and thy righteousness shall go before thee; the glory of the LORD shall be thy reward.

Then shalt thou call, and the LORD shall answer; thou shalt cry, and he shall say, Here I am. If thou take away from the midst of thee the yoke, the putting forth of the finger, and speaking vanity;

And if thou draw out thy soul to the hungry, and satisfy the afflicted soul; then shall thy light rise in obscurity, and thy darkness be as the noonday:

And the LORD shall guide thee continually, and satisfy thy soul in drought, and make fat thy bones: and thou shalt be like a watered garden, and like a spring of water, whose waters fail not.

And they that shall be of thee shall build the old waste places: thou shalt raise up the foundations of many *generations; and thou shalt be called, The repairer of the breach, The restorer of paths to dwell in.*

*If thou turn away thy foot from the sabbath, from doing thy pleasure on my holy day; and call the sabbath a delight, the holy of the LORD, honourable; and shalt honour him, not doing thine own ways, nor finding thine own pleasure, nor speaking thine own words:*

*Then shalt thou delight thyself in the LORD; and I will cause thee to ride upon the high places of the earth, and feed thee with the heritage of Jacob thy father: for the mouth of the LORD hath spoken it.*

---

I got my confirmation, and that led to two years of in-depth study in the Word about the historical observance of the church. We spent a lot of time in prayer over it, and we all agreed that we didn't want to miss the blessing if we chose not to observe one of the Ten Commandments. We got convicted that we were finding value in nine of the ten commandments and omitting one. We decided we wanted to obey them all, all ten of them.

---

Remember the Sabbath day by keeping it holy. Six days you shall labor and do all your work, but the seventh day is a sabbath to the Lord your God. (Exod. 20:8)

---

I should mention that for our entire marriage before our study, we called Sunday the Sabbath, but it was just a term we used for it. Other than going to church, we did not hallow the day or cease from work. We were workaholics, and rest was rare.

However, our household came into agreement about the day, and in 2010 we started to observe Saturday as the Sabbath. In Hebrew, it is called Shabbat. I realize you may have a different observance, and that is between you and the Lord. Seek Him in all His ways, and He will direct your path. I always say, obey where He guides! The reason I am sharing about this topic is because of the joy, peace, and health it has brought our family. Yes, health! We used to be a very sick family, but God set us free! I firmly believe that observing Shabbat as prescribed in scripture has been a big part of our complete physical and emotional healing. After all, the Word says there is a connection, and we believe the Bible contains truth!

---

**Then shall thy light break forth as the morning, and thine health (restoration) shall spring forth speedily. Isaiah 58:8**

---

The vital thing to note is that all my kids look forward to it too. It is now a personal conviction for them as well to observe it.

It's a family celebration day for us.

My daughters enjoy making traditional challah bread and baker's array for us on Erev Shabbat (Friday) to eat the next day. Scripturally, Shabbat starts on Friday at sundown. So as the sun goes down, we enter our rest. Our family begins to settle in for the night, and we look forward to a spiritually-based movie to watch. Since we usually stay up late, that means we sleep in really late. It is always great to wake up to our pre-made gourmet breakfast! As we eat, we read the Word and have an in-depth Bible discussion. Some of our sweetest family moments have been on our lazy Saturdays. We love to rest deeply and have Bible study conversations. Afterward, we usually find a church message to watch on the internet, and that always spurs on stimulating talks with all the kids. We can talk for hours. By the time our conversation is over, we usually are feeling full and sleepy, so we go back to sleep until about 4:00 p.m. Sometimes we take the kids to the park to play, and we always try to end our observance with communion. It's a beautiful family tradition that I feel is critical to establishing healthy family relations.

It's a blessing that my kids have said they want to observe Shabbat when they get married because they enjoy it so much. I define that as a legacy success! Not only do they love our time together, but they also enjoy growing in the Word as we enjoy a mostly unplugged (no devices) day together with no distractions.

Are you interested in establishing a Sabbath rest day?

Here are four ways to begin:

1. Stick to the heart of the Sabbath, which is rest. Take a mental and physical break.
   a. Cease from labor.
   b. Cease from worry.
   c. Cease from striving.

2. Unplug! We stay off social media and the internet unless I do a quick post to share our Sabbath meal to share the joy of Yahweh's command or to watch a message.
3. Sleep and sleep some more without guilt! Enjoy!
4. Prepare as much as possible on Friday.
   a. Cook meals that are easy to reheat.
   b. Use paper plates. A lot of people use nice dishes, but we take it easy.
5. Watch your favorite preacher or Bible message online.
   a. This is the only thing we usually watch on Sabbath day, and then we follow it with a discussion. My kids enjoy our family talks.

Remember, to focus on the goodness of the Lord. Leave all your cares and worries at the cross. It might be hard in the beginning, and if it is, ask yourself if you are having a hard time trusting Yahweh to cover you during your time off. Do you believe that He has everything under control even if you cease working for a day? When you realize what a true gift the Sabbath is, you can enter the rest it was intended to provide. The seventh day is the only day the Lord blessed, so it carries a blessing for those who observe it with a pure heart.

If you decide to celebrate Shabbat, please share your experience on a social media post with the hashtag #MOCShabbat and let us rejoice with you!

Shabbat is time to rest in the Lord

and soak in His presence.

—EmmaSara

# Ten Commandments

1. You shall have no other gods before me.
2. You shall not make for yourself an idol.
3. You shall not take the name of God in vain.
4. Remember the Sabbath day to keep it Holy.
5. Honor your father and mother.
6. You shall not murder.
7. You shall not commit adultery.
8. You shall not steal.
9. You shall not lie.
10. You shall not covet.

# Communion

When most people think of communion, they envision a church service, but we view it as an intimate time of fellowship and reconciliation.

---

*They worshiped together at the Temple each day, met in homes for the Lord's Supper, and shared their meals with great joy and generosity— Acts 2:46 (NLT)*

---

If you are under the assumption that this sacrament is limited to a church, please understand that there is no scripture stating it has to take place only in a church. The original communion took place in the upper room with a gathering of Christ's followers.

---

*And he took bread, and gave thanks, and broke it, and gave unto them, saying, This is my body which is given for you: this do in remembrance of me. (Luke 22:19)*

---

We break communion unleavened bread every week in our home. Our favorite time to take communion is on Sabbath. It's a beautiful way to end our day of total rest and family fellowship. We enter communion with my husband, saying a prayer, and sharing what he was grateful for during the week. We all look forward to it because it is such a positive time as we all take turns pointing out what went right in the week. Sometimes in life, we can feel like we are swimming against the current, and this simple tradition of sharing a moment of gratitude does the soul good. It also provides an opportunity to thank each other for any help we received from each other during the week, and everyone loves to feel appreciated.

It's easy for people to hold grudges against one another, month after month, year after year. Having a tradition to enter into communion allows us to prepare our hearts for the essential part of the evening, which is our time of reconciliation..

- However, it is our goal to reconcile and repent weekly for our wrongdoings.
o The scripture is clear that we need to confess our sins one to another. So this time is a perfect opportunity to cut down the root of bitterness, so it will not spring up in our home.
- We start our confession by saying, "Will you forgive me for?"
o We then name the offense to whomever we offended or hurt. It's a beautiful time of taking full accountability for our poor behavior or actions toward one another. It's a bridge-building time when the other person then responds, "I forgive you."
- After we are done repenting, my husband blesses the unleavened bread and grape juice, and we then we formally take communion as a symbol and recognition of what Christ did for us on the cross.

- o About once a month or as we are led, we turn our focus to Yahweh after we repent to one another.
- We invite the Spirit to search our hearts in case we sinned against Yahweh. It's a soul-cleansing time.
- After we purge our hearts, a sweet, sweet song fills the air as we all sing, "Nothing but the Blood of Jesus," together. It is such a holy moment in our home weekly.

On the rare occasion that we skip this tradition, the following week, the environment in our home can be on edge, and it seems tenser because we didn't get a chance to make things right, and our issues can quickly build up against each other. So, you know why we do it weekly.

How would you like to have a family tradition that ushers in forgiveness weekly and provides a place to be intimate with the one who died for your sins? Choose a day and time and make it a habit that you will change your relationships.

Communion is a beautiful time

of reconciliation and thanksgiving.

—EmmaSara

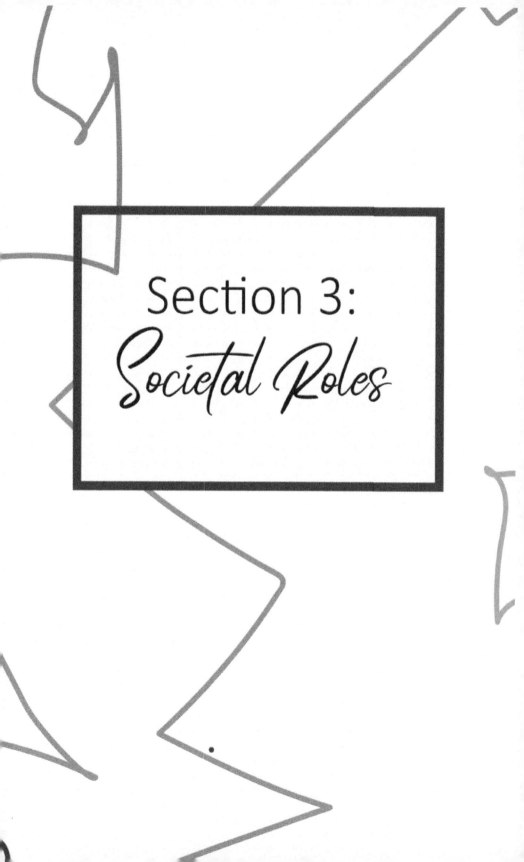

# Section 3:
## Societal Roles

# Chapter 8

# Parental Roles

# A Societal Look at Parental Roles

I don't believe one parent is more important than the other. I think each parent has a place in helping to form a child's worldview and personal identity.

As far as the impact of a father on a son's life: Studies show that boys who grow up in a fatherless home have a higher chance of ending up incarcerated.[6]

This reveals that the lack of a father's presence in a family can cause a son to have personal value issues, and it can stir up contention. As a former director of a women's shelter, when I asked my clients whether they would rather be fatherless or have a dysfunctional dad in their home, most clients would choose to have their dysfunctional dad home.

So what I learned over the years is that a child forms much of their value from their relationship with their dad—present or absent. When kids lack a father's love, they seek love and affirmation in all the wrong places — leading to teenage pregnancies for girls and sons seeking to belong. This lands many fatherless sons in prison and gangs. I realized that an imperfect and even angry (not specifically physically abusive) father in the home is better than none.

Growing up, my dad was young, so he had no idea how to communicate with me. I can remember as a teen; I could sneak out of the house while he was awake in the living room because he wouldn't check on me after he got home. Our communication wasn't too great, but I am so glad he was in my life with all of his imperfections. What he did right was that he stayed! He worked hard, he was ethical and was a good provider, and that was enough. I know if he could go back, a lot of changes would be made, but isn't that the plight of every parent who loves their kids? If you are in a relationship with the father of your children and you are considering divorce because you're not happy. Pray hard for wisdom because broken homes are the devil's playground. If your husband is safe for both you and your children press into God for growth in your marriage. Learn to appreciate the good you do have in your relationship for the sake of protecting your kids from statistical outcomes. If you are separated, pray about your child's relationship with their dad. Cover it in prayer. Leave bitterness at the cross and let Yahweh work creatively for the sake of your son or daughter.

Now let's look at the role of a mom in a child's life.

I believe what a mom gives to a child is the gift of nurture. From the 1828 Noah Webster's Dictionary:

---

*Nurture:*
*1. To feed; to nourish.*
*2. To educate; to bring or train up.*

---

286

After doing some research, I came across an email from a single mom who was responding to an article about a school shooting. It hits the heart of what I wanted to convey in this chapter. Kids need their mama in their life to teach them to be loving, kind, and respectful of life. But, most of all, they need nurture that only a mom can provide.

---

*"I was a single mom for five years. So when the father is missing from these boys' lives, so is the mother. Someone has to go out and provide, often working two or three jobs while the child stays in daycare or with a babysitter. With Mom being so tired when she gets home, she goes to bed. What the mass shooters did is wrong, but they probably never had anyone nurture them or love them. So really, when the provider is gone, so is the mother—the nurturing one. It's a sad epidemic."[7]*

---

I agree it's a sad epidemic when moms are absent from their kids' lives by choice or force. I understand many moms want to be more involved in their kids' lives, yet so many of them are absent to provide for their household out of survival, as we read above. If that is the case, pray the Lord would make-a-way for you to be with your kids. Don't forget to turn those prayers into thanksgiving as if it's already done. Turn those prayers into affirmations. Thank the Lord that He has opened doors for you to be present with your kids. Keep believing until it happens, keep decreeing. If you have to be away from them, create ways to stay connected to your kids. Utilize technology to be present, even if by video calls. When you are home, take time for your kids even when you are tired. Kids are so hungry for affection, and it doesn't take much to let them know you care. This is where nurture comes in; let them feel your genuine interest. If you are a single mom who feels concerned after reading this, please, ask the Lord for direction and peace. I know many adults raised by a single working mom who still felt very loved as kids, which is crucial. The bottom line is that kids need the love and nurture that only a mom can provide, so do your best to be present for your kids.

I know you want to do your best to raise your kids, but unfortunately, there are other moms who are severely un-nurturing by choice. This unloving behavior commonly leads to Reactive Attachment Disorder (RAD) in small children. It is far more damaging than if a child has a nurturing mom and is fatherless. RAD causes deep neurological dysfunction that carries into adulthood that can wreck a person's life forever! It can cause such radical brain dysfunction that people with RAD have been guilty of some of the world's most violent acts of crime. After working intensely with kids who had RAD, I can attest that once the damage is done, love is seldom enough to heal a child with RAD.[8]

It is challenging and sad. A child becomes a prisoner of circumstance because of the lack of nurture early in their life.

Why mention it? As a Mother of Change, it will benefit you to be aware of your surroundings and be educated about societal conditions.

When we understand the deep dynamics of parental roles, we can become empowered to understand what is going on in society. We can use our knowledge to survey who our kids are hanging around with because there is a saying, "hurt kids, hurt kids."

If a child suffers from RAD, they can be visibly "normal" but still be extremely dangerous, especially when left unmonitored. This book is your training manual to help keep your kids safe, so I had to include this topic. If you are thinking about adopting kids, I suggest reading *Parenting the Hurt Child: Helping Adoptive Families Heal and Grow by Gregory Keck first.* This book gives a candid look at dealing with behavioral issues that you should consider before adopting.

I should mention that it is possible to get RAD in other ways, like being subjected to neglect or abuse from another primary care provider. RAD generally happens within the first five years of life due to trauma or neglect. So be watchful of who is babysitting your kids, especially if they are with your kids more than you.

If you are reading this book, I believe that you have your child's best interest at heart. I want to declare to you that your mission is to be the nurturer of your home. Be loving, be watchful, and embrace the societal role that God ordained for you. It's an honor to be a mother.

It's an honor to

be a mother.

—EmmaSara

# Morality

As I mentioned earlier, I believe the future of our nation rests upon the shoulders of moms to bring change to our country. Why do I think that?

Because when moms allow immorality to rule in their homes, society will fail and become corrupt.

God's ways will be overlooked, and the nation will suffer.

In contrast, when moms uphold morality in their homes and raise kids with intentionality in the fear and admonition of the Lord, our nation will bear good fruit. Society will become a safer place to live.

Let's look at the subject of morality defined by the Webster's 1828 dictionary.

---

*Moral- Relating to the practice, manners or conduct of men as social beings in relation to each other, and with reference to right and wrong. The word moral is applicable to actions that are good or evil, virtuous or vicious, and has reference to the law of God as the standard by which their character is to be determined.*

---

Morality is on the decline in our nation, and stats show the USA is currently the number one consumer of sex worldwide. So we should pause and ask ourselves, what shifts had to take place within our nation to arrive at such a disappointing statistic?

---

*"The United States is the number one consumer of sex worldwide. So we are driving the demand as a society." -* — *Geoff Rogers, co-founder of the United States Institute Against Human Trafficking*

---

Warrior Queen, I am appealing to you right now. I am asking for your warrior spirit to rise up within you concerning this topic! Do not shrink back, and don't allow the enemy to keep you in the dark. Remember, I will say this repeatedly, satan loves naivety. He wants to keep you in the dark because he hates the light!

Darkness is exposed when we uncover the enemy's strategy to get us to play on his field. Remember, actions cause reactions; what we do ends with an outcome.

---

*Internet access without moral restraint + lust of the flesh + naïve people/parents= satan's playground*

---

Another area we need to consider is that every abuser or bully is someone's son or daughter. I mentioned before that no one thinks their kids are capable of committing crimes, but realize this, satan is, and he will tempt any kid to do bad things.

*"We found that the younger a man was when he first viewed pornography, the more likely he was to want power over women," Bischmann said.*[9]

The enemy is doing everything possible to breakdown family values. So let's look at his strategy so we can be on guard within our homes to stand against his satanic game plan!

## SATAN'S STRATEGY TO BREAKDOWN SOCIETY:

1.    Decrease parental authority over kids, which means creating legislation that decreases parental rights.

2.    Rewrite morality and disregard the Bible as the definer of righteous living.

3.    Convince parents to accept immoral acts as normal, especially within schools, libraries, kid's programs, and in movies.

4.    Aims to replace a Biblical mindset with a satanic mindset that views God's standards as unloving.

5.    Have schools teach children about sexuality early, including lewd acts that are too indecent to type out in this book!

6.    Entice children to get curious about sexual acts at a very early age, which can lead to children experimenting with other children sexually.

7.     Blur gender lines.

8.     Sexualize kids with clothing that is immodest and sexy.

9.     Create gender-neutral clothing lines so that parents vote with their money and buy into this corrupt system.

10.    Break up marriages in any way possible, including causing gender confusion within relationships in some cases.

11.    Entice kids to become addicted to violence in video games, movies, and books.

   a. Increase violence among kids via school shootings and bullying. Remember, guns are not the problem; the people being influenced by evil pulling the triggers are.

12.    Push pornography addiction.

13.    Decrease masculinity in males.

14.    Increase staunch feminism to oppose Biblical order.

15.    Systematically decrease the nurturing instinct among moms.

16.    Devalue and undermine the sanctity of life.

This list is by no means conclusive. It's just the tip of the iceberg concerning the enemy's plans.

So this brings me back to the heart of this topic. The Lord told me in prayer one day that when we protect our kids, we protect our nation.

- *We can accomplish this by safeguarding morality within our households and standing for upright legislation in government, within our communities, and in schools.*

Time is of the essence because boys are getting addicted to porn, younger and younger. Because of this adolescent character fail, kids are hurting kids at a higher rate.

The stats of first exposure to porn is alarming.

---

*"Studies show that the average age of first exposure was 13.37 years of age with the youngest exposure as early as 5."*[10]

---

If that isn't young enough, in one of my training classes, we learned that the average age a child begins to experience physical and sexual abuse is about six months of age. The reason for this starting age is because many moms re-enter the workforce about that time, and caregivers harm them. Too often, parents don't even realize what's happening to their child until something horrific shows. Remember the baby girl I mentioned earlier? She was only one when I noticed her signs, but her family was oblivious for around two more years until her caregiver was caught in the act!

Let's look at what we know.

*About 1 in 7 girls and 1 in 25 boys will be sexually abused before they turn 18.[4]*

*Ninety percent of the time children know the perpetrator, and 117 is the number of victims a perpetrator will likely have before being caught! As many as 40% of children who are sexually abused are abused by older or more powerful children. Juveniles are the offenders in 43% of assaults on children under age six.[5]*

Remember, I mentioned earlier that hurt kids, hurt kids. So watch who you allow your kids to play with and rethink sleepovers. I have heard more stories of inappropriate touching during sleepovers by cousins and friends than you want to know. We must make decisions daily to be on guard and not be naive of the plans of satan. Remember, he is a predator on the prowl looking for a child who is alone and impressionable. When you think everything is okay, he will strike and without notice! Keep this in mind the next time you're posting photos of your kids on social media in underwear or less: you immediately serve yourself up as a naive parent, and predators will take note. When our guard is down, the enemy will walk right in because we have left an open invitation for him.

With this in mind, we set guidelines for keeping our kids as safe as possible.

**Here are some of our SAFETY GUIDELINES:**

1. No sleepovers at all; hurt kids, hurt kids.
2. No kids are sitting on a man's lap.
3. No head tapping or petting our kid's head by males. Yes, we have had men try. One time tapping on the head will be noted, but the second time we speak up.
4. Men or teen boys are never allowed to be in a home where our kids are babysat. We haven't used a babysitter in years, but we still keep the rule.
5. Kids are not allowed to play with friends in the room with the door closed.
6. We are watchful of gifts given to our kids. We always look for any motives.
7. Gifts from strangers are never allowed.

For more reasons why we have our list check out these stats:

---

*FACT: Abusers often form relationships with potential victims and their families before the abuse. This is called "grooming."*

*Grooming is a process by which an offender gradually draws a victim into a sexual relationship and maintains that relationship in secrecy. At the same time, the offender may also fill roles within the victim's family that make the offender trusted and valued.*

---

Grooming behaviors can include:

• Special attention, outings, and gifts

• Isolating the child from others

- Filling the child's unmet needs

- Filling needs and roles within the family

- Treating the child as if he or she is older

- Gradually crossing physical boundaries, and becoming increasingly intimate/sexual

- Use of secrecy, blame, and threats to maintain control.[19]

This is also the reason why I do not change my baby's diaper in the open. We don't even expose a baby's nakedness because I have heard too many stories of babies getting molested that have haunted me for years! I am not going to serve my child to sexual predators that are like wolves in sheep's clothing who get thrills from uncovered children. Yes, you know these people, and yes, they can be other teens.

Yes, you trust them.

So, what can we do about this dilemma?

How can we improve child safety?

We must go after the demand. Sexualization and perversion is at the root of these violations, let's pluck up it up!

## Let's look at more facts:

Studies show that trafficking is working by the law of supply and demand. The higher the demand for children, the greater the supply that will be needed.

*"...the only way we're going to attack the supply side is by going after the demand. And that means the sex buyer needs to be held culpable for the damage and trauma that he or she is causing."*[10]

If the only way to make a difference in the supply is to go after the demand, this means culture must have a significant shift.

*Change needs to occur at home before we can see our nation reap the benefit.*

How will we achieve that?

1. We can help to re-establish morality in society by first taking personal inventory in our own daily lives. When we draw back to God's ways in our home, our country will reap the benefits.

2. Let us raise our family lifestyle standards to line-up with scripture.

3. Also, we need to stop enabling immoral behavior in our kids because they will grow up to become adults who impact society. Let us raise them to make a positive imprint.

We should work to be an example of righteous living in our communities. We also need to protect our children from being influenced by those who are opposed to biblical living. When we can re-establish morality in our homes, our nation will begin to show forth the good fruit.

So, mama, will you join the Mother of Change Movement and lock arms with other moms to stand against immorality in our nation? Will you protect your kids to in turn, protect our society?

*Our country is*

*depending upon you.*

# Take Action

What are 5 strategies the enemy uses to destroy society?

_____

_____

_____

_____

_____

What was the biggest surprise to you in this chapter?

_____

_____

What is the recipe for societal erosion?

_____

_____

_____

What can you do to create change and help to restore society?

_____

_____

_____

# Couples Divided

Unfortunately, the topic of division among spouses is one of the areas I deal with the most during my family strategy sessions. After many years of co-leading couples counseling, I can say that there are some efficient tools available to you and your husband to make your marriage better. However, the most effective marriage tool across the board is called death to self. If you are fed up with your marriage, and you don't feel a spark any longer, let me share an inside story with you about my marriage.

Let me warn you if you are in a relationship filled with marital bliss; my story might entice you to judge my marriage. If that is you, go ahead and skip this section and go to a topic that applies to you.

If you're ready for the story, let's go! I hope you leave this section encouraged!

I have been married for twenty-two years, and although I have a fascinating story of how we met, it wasn't the traditional love story. You know, guy meets girl, sparks go off, and they fall madly in love and get married. No, when I met my husband, he wasn't even my type! There was a zero lust factor involved. However, there was an attraction, but it was to Christ in him. I could see the light of Jesus shining inside him. I also could sense he feared God, and there was a spirit of humility about him. I was attracted to all those things. Deciding to marry him was a very logical decision. I was tired of dating men in the world and in the church, who were lust buckets, materialistic, and players!

When I met my husband-to-be, he was younger than my younger brother, and up until that time, I only dated older guys. He was handsome, just not my type. However, some months before meeting him, I told the Lord I was done with my shallow relationship list. I asked Yahweh to bring someone He thought would be best for me in a later season. I also made sure to let Him know I wanted a man that feared Him with a holy fear. I knew a man that feared him would know how to love me with an everlasting love. I knew a man that feared Yahweh wouldn't want to cheat on me out of his fear for God. I understand that a man that feared Yahweh wouldn't venture too far on a lost path because his reverential fear would lead him back to a place of repentance.

This is where our story begins... I was only twenty-three years old, and he was twenty. I met him in a church that doubled as a coffee house across the street from the boardwalk on the beach. Clinton had mechanical skills, and my best friend needed her car fixed, and he was looking to bless, so he offered to help. As my friend and I walked away from the quick chat, she gave me that look as if to say, "Hmm... this could be someone for you." She was taken and thinking of her girl, trying to hook me up! I smiled. I can remember looking back over at her and saying, "Thanks, but no thanks! I am not interested in a relationship right now; I'm done with guys. I'm trying to get my walk right with the Lord," and that was the end of that conversation. Some weeks went by, and I ended up hanging out a lot with Clinton and a group of church friends. One day, we were lying in the sand, soaking up the sun rays on the California beach. We were talking about our life history, when all of a sudden, out of nowhere, he pops out, "hey, I think I could fall in love with you."

Right then, I seriously heard the voice of the Lord, as if He was calling from heaven, "Don't distract him because I have a hedge of protection around him, and he is only to remain focused on Me in this season." I felt a holy fear come over me while I was lounging on the hot sand on that sunny day, and I turned over to look him directly in the eye with a straight face. I wanted to let him know I was serious, and I told him, "I'm not looking for a relationship. Besides, you need to focus on the Lord alone right now." He looked back out towards the ocean and nodded his head as if to say ok, and that was the end of that conversation.

Some time went by, and we were not romantic at all. One day he called to ask if he could come to my Bible study. Typically, in the past, I would have gotten excited about a guy wanting to attend a study with me, but that holy fear was still in me. I didn't know what to tell him except that it was an open study, so he could come if he wanted to. As soon as I hung up, I fell to the ground, and I asked God for mercy! I remember I earnestly cried out to God and said, "Oh Lord let my hands be clean. I didn't invite him, and this is a public meeting, but he is clearly coming for me; let it be far from me to deter his attention away from you!" As soon as I finished with an "Amen," the phone rang, and it was Clinton letting me know he just got this weird feeling that it wasn't right to attend. So he canceled and went to his regular Bible study instead. I felt relieved! But something extremely unexpected happened some weeks later. He called me while I was at work, and we had a brief talk. He was mentioning that it was a bummer that he had to leave in three short months to Greece, where he would be stationed for the military. I honestly don't remember any conscious thoughts about Clinton, except thinking that he was a standard for what Christian guys were supposed to be like. I also knew the Lord seriously had a covering over his life. I am not sure what happened that brought me to this point that I was on the phone with him, and without any forethought, as he was saying he was bummed he was leaving, I suddenly blurted out, "I want to go."

He made a long pause and repeated my words back to me; "You want to go?"

After a short pause, in a matter of fact way, I said, "Yeah, I want to go." Honestly, I don't know what the heck I meant.

I don't know if I meant... yeah, I want to escape from my life of just surviving while working three jobs, or if I was saying, I want to go with you to start a life. I'm not sure what my response was really about. As an overworked twenty-three-year-old, I do remember thinking that Greece sounded like a nice place to visit.

It was a moment in time that a single response would change the trajectory of my life forever! I found myself repeating it, with a slight question in my voice, "Yeah, I want to go." I think the tone helped me realize that I was just permitting myself to move forward with Clinton.

Before you know it, after a pause, I heard him say, "That means we would have to get married."

I didn't skip a beat and said, "Ok, but you will have to get my dad's permission first."

"Ok."

I said, "Ok, we can go to their house this weekend."

At this point, I was on my own and out of my parent's house for about four years. As a young woman, it wasn't common for me to ask my dad for permission to do things. However, the Lord did extensive work in my heart, and I knew I wanted to make things right with my dad before I got married. So, telling Clinton that he had to get my dad's permission first meant something so much deeper than he probably realized.

After knowing my dad for a total of three hours and losing multiple games of pool to him, he let my dad know why he was there. He asked my dad if he could talk to him, and at that moment, he "let the cat out of the bag" and asked if he could marry me. My dad was in disbelief because he thought is was a joke, but when he realized he was serious, he half laughed, "Ok... if you think you can handle her."

For years after that, whenever I was acting up, he would always tell Clinton, "I warned you!" Although I didn't always think it was funny in those raw moments being a newlywed, I can find some humor in it now.

My mom came home a couple of hours later, and when she came in, it was late, and she was tired. As she peered around the corner, she could see my guest, and she was not in the mood to meet anyone. She looked at me and said, "Not tonight." I felt my heart sink because I knew out of all nights this was the night I was hoping she would be in a good mood. We had a full house because my grandma was visiting too, and as I was sitting in the living room, he knelt down and proposed to me just minutes after my mom walked into the room!

And that's it; we lived happily ever after!

This is about the time you hear a record scratch, or in other words, the love tune stops. Our first year of marriage was a challenge as we got to learn more about each other. He wasn't like anyone I ever dated before. I was used to guys swooning over me, and my husband didn't seem overly interested in me like I thought a newlywed husband should. It was a surprise to me, but that lack of interest would go on for many years on both of our parts. I married him because he genuinely feared God, and that part never left him. How he lived that out changed from season to season; when he got a new job change, my husband changed. He was working in law enforcement in what we called the "devil's playground." His light seemed to grow dim, and since that is what initially attracted me to him, that affected our relationship immensely. His peers always knew him as a real deal Christian man, but I didn't see his fire for the Lord like his early days. As the years went by, we became extreme workaholics, and neither of us knew how to rest. For years, we never sat in our living room because there was no downtime for us. During that season, we only had three children because my husband was "done" having kids. We were still attending church, and I was very involved in ministry, plus I was always finding ways to make money while staying at home. We were like ships passing in the night for the majority of our marriage. Finally, the Lord started working in my husband's heart, and we had more kids. As I had more kids, it seems like I got involved in more projects. We didn't argue much because I tried not to give my husband things to complain about; I made sure that all my duties were taken care of, like keeping the house clean and organized, cooking all his meals, homeschooling the kids, taking care of our one-acre property, which included a large organic garden, and helped to remodel our home. I made sure to keep up on everything so he wouldn't have a reason to want me to stop my ministry involvements and entrepreneurial projects I was involved with during that time. I was a very driven person, and so was my husband. We were known as a very productive couple. So, *work became our common language.* We had work and loyalty in common, that and the fear of the Lord combined was the glue that held us tight over time.

Years would go by before the Lord allowed some life-changing circumstances to happen in our family that would lead to a hugely humbling experience. I write about the story in my book, *Passion. Purpose. Time Management.*

During all that busyness, it would take me years to realize that my husband dealt with cyclical depression. I didn't know the signs, and since he worked so much, I missed any clues. I didn't realize that working around the clock was a way that he self-medicated. It was a way for him to escape his emotions. For years our kids didn't see any public displays of affection.

As a matter of fact, they wouldn't encounter them as a norm until our twenty-first year of marriage!

Yes, it took over twenty-years for our marriage to bloom but bloom it did!

I finally fell in love with my husband in a more profound way! Our relationship went to a whole new level! According to my kids, we started acting like a real married couple. I mentioned that we didn't argue much for the majority of our marriage, but during the last four years of rediscovery, we had some of our biggest blowouts. I realized that we had a lot of unfinished business that had to be dealt with so we could move forward in our marriage. I feel like it meant that we were finally connected enough to express emotions towards each other. We are back to limited arguing, and life is sweet to be serving Yahweh from a position of marital strength and unity. We both equally desire to serve Yahweh and raise kids to become the change our world needs.

Even though our marriage has been lacking in a lot of areas, I have always loved him and cared for him deeply as the father of my children.

However, I didn't always feel 'passion' for him because I was frustrated with generational patterns in his life. Generational patterns are what we carry in from our upbringing and our DNA markers, both physical and spiritual. In other words, his baggage, his stuff.

His issues where...

## GENERATIONAL PATTERNS #1

1. Depression
2. Self-rejection
3. Victim Spirit
4. Withdraw

Let's face it; none of our baggage is attractive. Yes, I had my own unattractive qualities he had to deal with, which I list below.

My issues were...

## GENERATIONAL PATTERNS #2:

1. Pride
2. Anger
3. Rebellion
4. Frustration

It's easy to focus on our spouse's issues, but the truth is we all have areas that we need to surrender to God.

As you are reading, what comes to mind?

What is the Lord showing you about your generational patterns?

These two lists are not exhaustive. Each person has their own mix that they bring to the marital table.

I can remember being on fire for the Lord while Clint was going through a long season of emotional detachment. He hadn't left his faith, he always loved God, but the man was stuck. My husband had a traumatic childhood with a father wound that needed to be healed.

This left him committed to be the kind of dad that stayed with his kids, but he forgot that we needed him present emotionally too.

He wasn't always the spiritual leader I wanted him to be in our family. He would go through decent times and then detached seasons. Gratefully, I am not a needy woman, so I didn't require detailed attention, which was helpful because he wasn't at a place to offer it. Over the past two decades of talking to many married women, I noted the countless wives who had low self-esteem based upon how they felt their husbands treated them. I am talking about non-abusive marriages; marriages were husbands were not attentive in their marriage. In our marriage, I defined what a good husband was early on our relationship, and I felt that my husband fit that definition. Because I did this as a new bride, I was able to keep high self-esteem and personal strength.

What was my definition of a good husband?

**A GOOD HUSBAND**

1. Fears God
2. Loyal
3. Good Provider
4. Respectful

Whenever I felt myself growing weary of his generational patterns, I found myself being grateful for any one of the above areas on my "good husband" list.

I do want to mention during that long season; I made sure not to entertain the thought of divorce even though the enemy sent temptations my way! I always knew it was better to stay together then think about leaving because I couldn't bear the thought of remarrying a man that could potentially harm my kids. I have heard too many sad stories from friends and family members of boyfriends or new husbands' violations.

**Violation is defined: child molestation, spousal abuse, pornography addiction, verbal abuse, etc.**

I have always been very protective of my kids, so I still count the cost when their safety is at stake. The truth is that many women get divorced from their husbands only to remarry another man like the previous one they left. So, they end up with compounded potential problems, including children enduring emotional trauma; some kids are violated by boyfriends/husbands/new friends, others are emotionally abused by new boyfriends or girlfriends spurred on by jealousy.

It's a lie from satan that the grass is greener on the other side. With that in mind, I stayed devoted to my marriage. I kept my fear of the Lord in my heart, and I recognized that satan loves divorce! With all those variables listed above, it's no wonder why he does.

As a Mother of Change, my goal has always been to do what is best for my kids. I chose to look in the mirror, and I found myself humbled and repentant for all my unsavory and ungodly ways.

As a mom, there were a lot of things I was doing right, but as a wife and a child of God, I had secrets. However, the Lord was dealing with my heart and my inner workings. In my self-check time, my secrets were revealed; I was found to be pharisaical, controlling, and operating out of a religious spirit at times. In 2010, after being married for thirteen years, the Lord humbled me in a big way. It was a dark time for our family, but from death sprung life. The Lord will indeed allow us to hit rock bottom so that we can reach the end of ourselves.

Things improved after 2010, but our marriage still had many issues that we needed to work through. My husband had to gain self-love by surrendering his childhood wounds to Yahweh, and I had to learn to die to self by putting pride to death.

Finally, in our twenty-first year of marriage, I got a new husband! Really new! Our family even legally changed our last name to a historical family name. My husband wanted a fresh start, and that meant taking on a new name. During this significant change in my husband's life, we found out that there was a mistake on a historical document, and his last name was spelled wrong. McMillan was incorrect. It was the perfect time to change his name! He decided to take on the original spelling from his great grandfather Abraham McMillion, a man of God. My husband renounced generational curses and spiritual DNA riders and broke free! ,He decided to choose to step into becoming a new man.

If you are wondering how this all came about, I had a full strategy for many years that I share during my Family Strategy Consultation Sessions.

Part of the strategy included: Writing down affirmations for my husband.

Make a journal and write out ten affirmations for your husband.

## 10 AFFIRMATIONS for Him

Insert his name below or create your own affirmation list.

1. _____ fears the Lord.
2. _____ is loyal.
3. _____ respects my counsel.
4. _____ is a good listener.
5. _____ and I are in love.
6. _____ is a good example for our kids.
7. _____ makes sure the kids respect me.
8. _____ values me and my work.
9. _____ and I have great communication.
10. _____ and I are united in raising the kids.

Once you have those ten affirmations down for your marriage, turn your daily focus to yourself.

Concentrate on personal growth because...

*The greatest strength you have is the power to change yourself.*

You can't make your spouse change, believe me, I tried and pushed. However, that just stunted the process.

So, focus on you. Start a plan for self-improvement: mind, body, and spirit. Ask yourself, "how can I be a better mom and spiritual covering for my kids?" Take your eyes off everything your husband is not doing and take care of the things you can personally improve. Also, stop worshipping your husband. If you are expecting him to fill your heart up, you are worshipping him. I didn't worship my husband, and he definitely didn't worship me. This was a spiritually safe place to be. I know too many wives who want their husbands to fulfill only what God can provide. Yahweh is a jealous God, so beware of desiring from your husband what the Spirit wants to meet in your life. Remember, whatever you start your relationship with becomes its foundation! So if you begin with lust it's easy to slip into worshipping your spouse. If you entered into a relationship with that as the base, you will never find peace within your marriage until you stop worshipping him. Another form of worship is desiring of your husband, what only Yahweh can provide. If you put an over-emphasis on what you expect from your husband emotionally or even spiritually, you can be treading on dangerous ground.

When a person is very broken, it's easy to become consumed with wanting to be filled by a spouse. However, Yahweh is a jealous God and He will not allow you to get from your husband what He wants to provide for you first. So let your cup be filled with Christ and His love first.

Like I said, my husband was emotionally unavailable. My husband rarely thanked me for my work, he rarely told me I was attractive, and there were many times he told me he was unhappy. All that could have broken many women, but I never let it break me. I never took ownership of his brokenness. I was immovable and emotionally stable because my value was set forth by God. Christ was my everything, and my private worship time with Him was intense. I knew I was not perfect, but I knew I wasn't the problem, it was the victim spirit that was to blame. So I turned my focus to that spirit, which was at work. I went on a mission to help my family be set free, especially my husband. I pressed in. I prayed. I proclaimed. I listened to the spirit and I obeyed, and my husband and my family got free. We got free from health problems. We got free from generational junk! Because we remained together, we succeeded together! It took twenty years of patience, but it was worth the work and the wait!

All the prayers and proclamations I said for so many years came to pass! He became who I said he was.

I proclaimed that:

- He would be a man after Yahweh's heart like David.
- He would have the boldness of Paul the apostle.
- He would have the wisdom of King Solomon.

My private words became a reality. He became steadfast for Christ. He is not ashamed of the gospel, and he has lead successful men's counseling for some time. Now, we stand united, raising our kids in the way of the Lord. I believe living in family unity is Yahweh's gift to society; it the sweetest way to live.

If the Spirit moves you, reflect, take time to stop, repent, and ask Yahweh to show you affirmations to say over yourself and your husband. One of my daily affirmations is that I am an honoring wife.

Whenever I overstep a personal boundary by acting contrary to my affirmation, I backstep, repent, and make things right by changing my attitude.

I choose to get back on track. I acknowledge that if I don't, I am partnering with satan to destroy my family, and I reject his plan!

## FOUR DAILY AFFIRMATIONS

I am:

1.  An honoring wife.
2.  Quick to listen.
3.  Slow to anger.
4.  Humble.

The bottom line is that life begins to change when we look in the mirror and focus on improving ourselves: mind, body, and spirit. Once we begin to experience transformation, we can have more grace for others. Finally, don't forget to fast and pray for unity in your marriage. It is a powerful tool for change!

# Take Action

What are your immediate thoughts after reading this chapter?

_____

_____

_____

_____

Now stop, pray, and ask God about what He wants you to apply after reading this chapter. Write out your answer.

_____

_____

_____

_____

_____

What 2 affirmations will you speak over your husband daily in your quiet time alone?

_____

_____

I am powerful.

I create change!

—Emma Sara

# Single Role

Mama, no matter how you arrived at your current circumstance, I want to encourage you. This past month the Lord has put you on my mind and heart in a profound way. The Lord has seen your struggles and heard your prayers. He knows you are tired. He knows you are stressed. He knows you want more for your family. You are carrying the weight of not only being a solo parent but, most likely, the exclusive provider of your household. I understand that it's hard not to feel overwhelmed with the daily grind, but the Lord has not forgotten you. Just think of it this way: you have the unique opportunity to lean on Jesus Christ as your husband and provider. He is so much more reliable and faithful than any human being could ever be. He wants you to lean into Him. Maybe you are forced to work outside of the home when you desire to be home with your kids. Don't give up hope. Call heaven down to earth! Live a life that is sold out for Christ.

Trust in Him in all your ways, and not only will He direct your path, but He will also make a way where there seems to be no way!

He will bring water from a rock, and He will make streams run in the desert for you.

- If single-parent homes are common in your family, break off family curses, especially cut off the poverty spirit.

- Decree that you are not subject to the enemy's plan for your life!
- Decree that you are a daughter of the Most High King and that you will sit in high places where there is great protection and provision for your family.
- Then make sure to CHANGE your life patterns.
- Don't continue and do business as usual.

Also, ask the following things in Prayer:

1. Ask the Father for a new blueprint for your life.
2. Ask the Holy Spirit to reveal broken systems and broken mindsets.
3. Ask for the ability to have unobstructed vision and hearing to the things of God.

Do you find yourself concentrating on obstacles rather than the blessings in each day? Stop rehearsing the pain. Stop rehearsing defeat. Start proclaiming what you want to see as if it were. Speak those things as if though they are. (Rom. 4:17) With expectation, start declaring gratitude for what will be placed in front of you as if you just sat down at the Lord's banquet table. I think of the historical story of George Mueller, who was responsible for orphans. He would sit at a large table with hungry orphans all around and wait on God. One particular story vividly stuck out to me:

*The children are dressed and ready for school. But there is no food for them to eat, the housemother of the orphanage informed George Mueller. George asked her to take the 300 children into the dining room and have them sit at the tables. He thanked God for the food and waited.*

*George knew God would provide food for the children as he always did. Within minutes, a baker knocked on the door. "Mr. Mueller," he said, "last night I could not sleep. Somehow, I knew that you would need bread this morning. I got up and baked three batches for you. I will bring it in." (Georgemueller.org)*

---

Their Daddy (God) provided for them continually! So turn your focus to heaven and concentrate on Jesus being your provider and heavenly husband! Remind yourself that His resources are unlimited, and His favor is abundant. All He wants is your trust, and He longs for a relationship with you. On the other hand, the enemy wants you to feel alienated, alone, and without support.

Line up your faith with the Lord's prayer.

---

**"Thy kingdom come, Thy will be done in earth as it is in heaven! Give us this day our daily bread!" (Mat. 6:10)**

---

Jesus taught us how to pray. He gave us the prayer blueprint that moves mountains and provides manna on the daily for us. So don't lose hope. Use this time to see God move in a way that many people don't experience because they have their needs easily met. I understand what it feels like to be in a place of total trust in God for daily provision. Our family hit a poverty-level income for a season, and we were left to flex our faith muscles or crumble under the day-to-day stress. A string of events occurred that left us without a salary and benefits while we lived in an RV with a family of ten! When our finances were the bleakest, we became the most resolved to trust God. Sure, we struggled big time, but we continued to course-correct our attitudes, and we had to decide to appreciate the struggle. We learned that Yahweh was using our trials to bring refinement in our lives so we could learn to have total dependence upon Him.

Our lifestyle was a lot like living in a past era or another country. When we moved to our property, we had no electricity, which meant my husband had to run super loud generators all day. They were so loud you could barely hear each other. We also had no running water for a long time, so we had to haul water. There were plenty of days we had no water at all. After living in our RV for so long, things started to break down systematically, and our drains were continuously getting backed up, which meant foul order. The worst part was we couldn't keep the windows open because many days, we had high winds, and since our property had a lot of loose dirt, we couldn't leave the windows open.

During that season of lack, we witnessed more miracles in four years than many people will experience in a single lifetime. Although there was nothing fun about not knowing exactly where gas money or food would come from week to week, I wouldn't trade that season for anything. Why? Because I had the privilege of mirroring my kids what it looked like to walk through life's difficulties and challenges and still trust God. They got to participate in trusting God. They prayed and then watched Him provide much more abundantly than we could ever think or imagine! For the rest of our life, we will have campfire stories of all the ways

Yahweh provided for us in supernatural ways. So, be encouraged! God's got you! This is the time to break out of the old and step forth into the new. New wine can't be put into old wineskins because they will burst (Mark 2:22)! So if you want a new life choose a new way of thinking, a new way of viewing yourself, a new way of viewing men. Most importantly, trust God in a new way.

# Take Action

Lessons I learned EmmaSara's testimony:

_____

_____

Two questions to ask God in prayer concerning my
marriage:

_____

_____

_____

Do you have family curses to break off?

_____

_____

_____

Areas to trust God with:

_____

_____

_____

_____

_____

# Does It Take a Village?

There is a common saying, "It takes a village to raise a child," and I have heard the phrase used increasingly in more recent years.

This topic piqued my interest, and I was curious about what God had to say about the subject. I pressed into prayer and decided to research what the Bible had to say about it. When I studied this topic, it was clear that the families lived in village communities in biblical times. This wasn't a surprise finding. It just reinforced that raising a child in a village would have been considered normal in Bible times.

However, I have not technically raised my kids in a village environment for the past twenty-one years of marriage.

As a matter of fact, I have been guarded against external influences on my family.

I have been very selective about their friends, and I have taught them to watch their friend groups. As the saying goes, "Show me your friends, and I will show you your future." By discernment, we must approve the friends they do have. Most of their friend base is formed through long-distance relationships, and they only see some of their friends on an annual basis. How do my kids feel about this? They consider me and my husband their best friends, and that feels great! My oldest son is always quick to say that he doesn't need another best friend besides his dad. Yes, he is a daddy's boy even though he is eighteen. My son loves his father and respects him highly. I understand some will call into question the area of socialization, but if you are around my kids even for a short amount of time, you will find that they function well around all walks of life in a friendly, confident manner. My kids are social butterflies. They have no fear of talking to kids or adults and get this; my kids are genuinely interested in having deep conversations.

So back to the village concept.

This got me thinking, "Does it really take a village to raise a child?"

With a family of ten, it sure feels like a village sometimes, but I haven't leaned on an external friend or family group to help raise my kids.

I have been incredibly intentional in all that we do as a family, producing thriving, dynamic, healthy human beings. I didn't say perfect, but they are well-rounded. They are very friendly and genuinely interested in the needs of others. Much of society has an "anything goes" village mindset rather than an intentional one. Yet the fruit will reveal if the root is good, and I see many self-focused individuals around, which leads to a selfish culture.

However, I do recognize an "intentional village" support system is hugely beneficial for some families. I would define an "intentional village" as a societal group with unity in faith, morals, and conduct. While I see the benefits of living in a like-minded community, I wouldn't say it is mandatory to raise godly, healthy, happy children.

I am under the precept that satan is a liar and that he has come to kill, steal, and destroy the family (John 10:10).

He would love us to live counter to God's best for us. He hates God's ways. So I am always on guard for his lies. Remember, Adam and Eve, were in a perfect garden. They could have lived in bliss if they hadn't believed a lie.

In her promo spot, Melissa Harris-Perry, a former political commentator for NBC said:

---

*We have to break through our kind of private idea that kids belong to their parents, or kids belong to their families, and recognize that kids belong to whole communities.*[13]

---

Warrior Queen, any statement like the one above should provoke holy anger within you! This is the same kind of ideology that strips loving, caring parents of their children because they are not conforming to governmental edicts that harm our children rather than protect them. There are so many stories of newborns being ripped away from parents at birth because they elected a gentle approach to care for their babies. Loving parents and new babies experienced trauma because of hospital standards. I guarantee you that more damage was done by ripping that babe away then leaving them with their parents without one-shot or eye cream! Many times, kids are taken away from parents for not adhering to educational standards only to be put into foster care where they are molested. When a state is trying to make vaccinations mandatory, even if a child has a sound medical reason to object, it is clear they do not have our children's best interest in mind. When a government thinks they own our children, it is an indicator that they are pawns in satan's hands to perform his unholy work in our nation!

Oh, the torture of a mother's heart! I am not advocating that vaccines are never necessary; that's not an argument I am trying to stir up in this book. As a loving parents, we should have the right to make decisions for our children that will protect their lives and health without government intervention. Why? Because they are our children, not the government's.

We use the Bible as our fulcrum measure to balance out our lives and to make sure our family stays on track. When I reviewed Biblical history, I noted that God's people, Israel, lived in villages that were tightly monitored with set standards for the entire nation. Even before Israel was a nation, it's clear that Yahweh had a moral standard for His people. The tribe or "family" of Israel had clear guidelines for their villages. They were to live in unity and be in one accord in faith and belief in Yahweh, plus be observant of the same laws. The whole of the law was to be the same for strangers that entered the camps too. Paganism or pagan customs were not permitted to be practiced in the villages. Yahweh even provided a book of standards/laws, so there would be no excuse for them not to live righteously. Of course, as history reveals that even with all Yahweh did to establish these villages as set apart, there were still those who tried to fulfill the lust of the flesh. But it is important to note that the Lord never allowed behavior counter to His Torah and His laws. He didn't lower the standard or the law just because some people were obstinate toward it.

This got me thinking about our current culture and how many moms are handing over their power and parental authority daily by allowing an ungodly village to partner in raising their kids. It was never part of Yahweh's plans for His children to integrate with pagan customs. He set clear standards for His society and villages. As a Mother of Change, I desire to live according to the Word, and in doing so, I know I can look forward to the blessings of God because all His ways are right. When it comes to village talk, ask yourself, am I raising my kids in the camp (schools, youth groups, friend groups, mom groups, and so on) of the enemy, or are they united in Spirit, truth, and conduct? You may notice I mention youth groups. Yes, the enemy can even use them to infect your children. Ask me how I know. I was a teenager going to a youth group that I later found out had an adulterous youth leader. It was no wonder he couldn't call out the youth group members for drinking and smoking pot during our service breaks!

I am not saying that we should live in caves or hide our children from society. I take my kids around the USA with me, and they are around a lot of people groups, but they have been raised with high intention and a covering of biblical and godly instruction. So many societal villages are like Sodom and Gomorrah. They reject the ways of Yahweh and ostracize our kids and prevent them from freely practicing their faith. They preach inclusion, but they wholly reject God's laws and any opinion that does not agree with their own. It's hypocrisy, and they expect people to comply, or they will bully and intimidate parents with threats. Oh, the threats! They can be fierce. The anger and the harshness should be a red siren for you. Don't ignore the siren! Danger! The danger for you and your children!

You can't raise your kids in Sodom and expect them not to be negatively influenced. Sodom was a biblical town that was full of people that went astray. The town became so saturated with sin that there were not enough righteous citizens to preserve the city from being spared from destruction. It was utterly destroyed along with every person, young and old alike—decimated. This reminds me of a scripture that says,

---

"A little leaven leavens the whole lump" (Gal. 5:9 NKJV)

---

In baker talk, to make bread, it only takes a little yeast to cause a lump of dough to rise, or in other words, to be significantly impacted. In the same way, if we have our kids around peer groups filled with leaven (ungodly behavior), we shouldn't expect them not to be impacted, or in this case, infected!

Be ready to ask Yahweh, "Am I raising my kids in a way that glorifies you, Lord?" Seek God about your village influence. Let the Holy Spirit be your guide. Be open to His best direction for your family and watch spiritual growth spring up in your home like never before.

# Take Action

Two things I learned about the Village mentality:

_____

_____

_____

Do you believe kids belong to their parents or the government?

_____

_____

How have you been raising your kids? With a village or without?

_____

_____

_____

If so what kind of village is it? Intentional or anything goes?

_____

_____

_____

*On parenting, repeat:*

*I have what it takes to raise kids*

*that will change the world!*

# Our Civil Commission

*Therefore, I exhort first of all that supplications, prayers, intercessions, and giving of thanks be made for all men, for kings and all who are in authority, that we may lead a quiet and peaceable life in all godliness and reverence. (1 Tim. 2:1 KJV)*

Scripture makes it clear we are to regularly be praying and interceding for officials and heads of state. Can you imagine what this nation would be like if people spent more time praying and proclaiming over legislation instead of complaining and ranting?

In the following pages, you will learn how to get your family up to speed in serving our country spiritually and with your vote!

## Teaching Kids to Respect Authority

I realize there are some hot topics covered in this book. However, it's not my desire to purposely push buttons for the sake of debate. I think people should have the autonomy to make their own decisions. We should not be forced to do things against our conscience, especially regarding how we lead our homes. There are societies like that, and they are called dictatorial.

As believers in Christ, we revel in the freedoms His sacrifice afforded us. Yet even with all our independence, we still have boundaries and extensive instruction in how we are to conduct ourselves toward those in authority and within society. God uses boundaries, order, and structure to create order in society.

---

**Let every soul be subject to the governing authorities. For there is no authority except from God, and the authorities that exist are appointed by God. (Rom. 13:1)**

---

Let's look to the Word for how we are to respond to authority, especially when it comes to leadership we don't agree with. If you are looking to do a dig deep with your family, study the topic of government in the Bible. Our family studied the subject for about three years, and we all learned so much. If you want to learn how to keep God first in our nation, I highly suggest the study because it teaches a proper worldview about governmental systems.

There always will be officials in authority that we disagree with, but we must remember to remain respectful in our conduct. I know it can be hard, but the Bible gives us an example of how we are to treat rulers that God establishes. Remember, we don't have to respect a person's actions, especially if they are contrary to God, but we do have to respect the position.

An insightful Biblical example is David's story and his response to King Saul after the Spirit of the Lord left him. An evil spirit vexed Saul, and he was set on murdering David out of jealousy. Yet after all the times King Saul pursued David to kill him, David kept his heart pure toward him and gave him the utmost respect.

---

*Then the men of David said to him, "This is the day of which the LORD said to you, 'Behold, I will deliver your enemy into your hand, that you may do to him as it seems good to you.'" And David arose and secretly cut off a corner of Saul's robe. Now it happened afterward that David's heart troubled him because he had cut Saul's robe. And he said to his men, "The LORD forbid that I should do this thing to my master, the LORD's anointed, to stretch out my hand against him, seeing he is the anointed of the LORD." So David restrained his servants with these words, and did not allow them to rise against Saul. And Saul got up from the cave and went on his way.*
*(1 Sam 24:4-7)*

---

David had plenty of reasons to attack the king while he was in a vulnerable position. Yet David would not allow his men to harm him because he acknowledged that it's Yahweh that sets a man in a seat of authority. He respected the position and would not even speak negatively against the one that was trying to destroy him. What a lesson to learn!

David did what was right in Yahweh's eyes. It's hard to understand how some evil men can get into places of position but know this: God does not sleep. He does not slumber. As a matter of fact, in some cases, He will set an evil ruler over a nation as a form of judgment against an obstinate people.

So what is the proper response to officials that we find to be offensive or immoral in personal conduct?

Try to concentrate on what they are executing for God.

We must ask God:

1. Are they an agent of judgment on this nation because of rebellion toward Yahweh?
   a. If you believe so, pray for our nation to repent and for God to have mercy on us!
2. Are their personal behaviors lacking, but their civil duties lining up with the biblical government?
   a. If so, pray for their salvation and that they repent and get their household in order.

Doing this will help you see and without offense, which can be a large blinder to God's hand at work in or through an individual.

We don't have to like or even agree with what a certain authority figure does, but we should honor the position.

If we are truly troubled with an official, we need to commit to the following:

1. Praying for them often. My favorite thing to do is to proclaim things as if though they are in the present tense. In other words, thank God in advance for things, even if they aren't a reality yet. If we want our president to be more sensitive to public needs, we need to

proclaim it out loud instead of murmuring and ranting about it. We say thank you that our president is.... The enemy probably laughs when we get stuck complaining about what we don't like, rather than launching forth in intercession. It's not only ineffectual for change, but it also adds kindling to the fire!

2. Follow government and state guidelines for letting our voice be heard, including calling state representatives with your verbal vote on bills often!

3. Make sure we vote on legislation and elections.

4. Pray for a God-fearing replacement if you feel they are opposed to God.

For about two years, my drive to the closest grocery store was about forty minutes, which meant that I would do the long haul anytime I needed the smallest thing. During the trip, I would enjoy my time calling heaven down to earth! (Matt. 6:10)

In other words, instead of worrying about what I didn't agree with, I would give verbal thanks out loud for things that were going right.

I would:

- Proclaim things as if they were already happening.
- Thank God that my parental rights will never be taken away.
- Thank Yahweh for raising up God-fearing legislators.

In other words, I used that time to pray not only for my family but also for our nation. I can't tell you how many times the very things I decreed came to pass!

Next time you're tempted to complain, try the practice of blessing and praying instead. It will be good for you and helpful for our nation. If certain people are foul and evil and it seems there is no good in them, pray a covering over our nation. Pray for them to be removed from office and replaced with someone that fears Yahweh and has reverence for Him. Ask for a swift movement. As I mentioned above, sometimes the Lord places evil individuals into authority as a judgment against people for rejecting Him and his ways. In this case, you should pray for the repentance of the people that would usher in such atrocities because of their godless behavior. Pray that the ungodly would be uprooted from high places, but leave vengeance to God. For it is written, "Vengeance is mine," says the Lord. Remain obedient to God and be cautious with your complaints, understanding that it is God that puts people into office, for it is written, "Do not touch My anointed ones." This makes me think of King Cyrus of Persia who did not know Yahweh, yet he was in fact, anointed to do God's good work for His children.

---

*Thus says the LORD to His anointed, To Cyrus, I have even called you by your name;*

*I have named you, though you have not known Me. (Isa. 45:1, 4)*

---

Queens, let God be God, and let us be obedient and wise as serpents and as gentle as doves! He has established boundaries, orders, and structures. Let us conduct ourselves decently and in order.

You are a Warrior Queen, and you know the battle is won on your knees! So get praying! The Lord glories in this form of combat!

# Take Action

Why should you teach your child to respect authority?

_____

_____

_____

_____

What is your civil responsibility as a mother and child of God?

_____

_____

God's ways are framed with these three things:

_____

_____

_____

What is your plan to help support righteous government?

_____

_____

_____

# Proclamations for Officials

Prayer changes things. Prayer changes our nation! So, don't forget to pray for our president weekly or as much as possible!

---

Father, I thank you that our president:
Fears you with a holy reverential godly fear. (Heb. 12:28)

---

- His heart is in your hands like rivers of water that you direct. (Prov. 21:1)
- Seeks godly counsel and wisdom in all things. (James 1:5)
- Acknowledges that he is in office because you placed him there. (Dan. 2:21)
- Surrounds himself with God-fearing wise counselors. (Prov. 20:18)
- Hates evils and clings to what is pure, holy and righteous. (Rom. 12:9)
- Makes God-honoring decisions based on the Word particularly in the areas of the preservation of life, marriage, and protection of parental and religious freedoms. (Exod. 20)
- Seeks to glorify God in all his ways. (1 Cor. 10:31)

I encourage you to proclaim this list over both men and women in high places as often as possible.

I can remember when all my kids were small, we had a prayer list, and each day we had a specific people group to pray over. One day was reserved for our president, legislation, and legislators.

If you are interested in making mountains move in the spirit, start your own list.

Here is an inspiration list:

1. Monday- Government/political issues
2. Tuesday- Unsaved friends/family members
3. Wednesday- Protection of small children
4. Thursday- Your household needs
5. Friday- Against sex trafficking
6. Saturday- Shabbat as the Lord leads
7. Sunday- Church congregation and leadership

It's never too late to start a good habit. So I encourage you to commit to pray for officials once a week with your kids.

What is your commitment?

I will pray _____ for the President and our government during this period of time _____.

Sign _____ Date _____

**Keep your word to yourself and our nation.**

# Voting

Life can get busy, but we need to keep our eyes and ears open when opportunities come up to vote. Please, remember that the media's job is to sway you to believe their narrative about candidates; this is called propaganda. If you watch liberal news, you will get anti-conservative, defaming news about candidates. Of course, it can go both ways. It comes with politics. I don't like to be put into boxes, so I don't like placing party labels on myself, so all I can say is that *I vote in accordance with the Bible*. I vote based upon my convictions to uphold God's directive for government in our nation. There are plenty of scriptures to help us understand how to place our votes. The Bible is not politically correct. Jesus was not politically correct. As a matter of fact, the Savior of the world was rejected even by the religious circles' heads. So, voting Biblically can get people upset, but it's before God and God alone do I stand or fall.

I refuse to tell Him, on the last day, when I meet Him face to face that I was just trying to vote politically correct. We will all have to give an account for our choices. I live to Christ, and I vote according to Biblical principles. I included a voting guide that I created, you may find the list separated in a partisan way, and I can not help that. I made it based upon the Word; I vote a political standard, not a specific party. I vote to keep Yahweh's rule in our government. I will be very candid when I say that the enemy wants a satanic government. He is after our nation. We have a clear portrait of what satanic influence looks like in government by taking a look at history. Some names that come to mind are Hitler, Saddam Hussein, and Fidel Castro the Latin socialist.

---

### Socialist Satanism in the Nineteenth Century

*Starting with the English Romantics at the end of the eighteenth century, European radicals developed a discourse of symbolic Satanism, which was put to use by major names in socialism like Godwin, Proudhon, and Bakunin. This shock tactic became especially widespread in turn-of-the-century Sweden, and accordingly the article focuses on the many examples of explicit socialist Satanism in that country. They are contextualized by showing the parallels to, among other things, use of Lucifer as a positive symbol in the realm of alternative spirituality, specifically the Theosophical Society. A number of reasons for why Satan gained such popularity among socialists are suggested, and the sometimes blurry line separating the rhetoric of symbolic Satanism from actual religious writing is scrutinized.* [20]

---

Mama, the Spirit has been making it very clear to me this week that He is looking for **RADICAL Mothers of Change**. Why? Because satan is radical. It's time to counter his work. Forms of radical political ideologies include *socialism* (far left) and *fascism* (far right).

Radical is defined as:

*Going to the root or origin.* (Dictionary.com)

The enemy is united and militant to attempt to uproot Biblical values in our government and nation. So, we must be radical in response to such acts by countering to satanic legislation from our nation. Let's take a further peek into the enemy's locker room.

There is a political sector called the radical left-wing.

**The radical left** may refer to several political families:

*The most radical part of Left-wing politics:*
*Anti-capitalism*
*Far-left politics*
*Political radicalism*
*Ultra-leftism 21*

Anti-capitalism is another term for a socialist system. Remember, socialism is a satanic political system. Why? Because socialism is atheistic and opposed to Yahweh. Karl Marx is known for his writings in the Communist Manifesto; he is also widely accepted by many as the father of socialism. He was open about his opposition to religion. Remember, we are in the business of getting to the destructive ROOT because it will show forth fruit if we don't pull it up.

*Religious suffering is, at one and the same time, the expression of real suffering and a protest against real suffering. Religion is the sigh of the oppressed creature, the heart of a heartless world, and the soul of soulless conditions. It is the opium of the people.*

*The abolition of religion as the illusory happiness of the people is the demand for their real happiness. Karl Marx*

*(History of Socialism en.wikipedia.org)*

---

He said religion is the opium or drug of the people!

And in laymen's terms, he stated above, the end of religion as imaginary happiness of the people is the demand for their real happiness (*emphasis added*).

In other words, putting a stop to religion would provide real satisfaction for the people! Danger! Danger! Why would we want this ideology at the forefront of our government system? They parade as an "angel of light" as a political party for the people, but the end is death!

And no wonder, for Satan himself masquerades as an angel of light.

---

*(2 Cor. 11:14 NIV)*

---

You might be thinking, wait EmmaSara, you just mentioned they are openly anti-God, how is this a masquerade? "Angel of light" is defined as acting in favor of the people or for the good of mankind. While these people are open about being anti-God, they still entice people with a false utopia that has a hellish end.

350

So your eyes are probably open now that you have read all of this, but many people don't see satan with his angel costume on, all they see is a group of people pushing power to the working people. They promote equality, but to what end? As in where does it lead us, and what is the result? Just look at many other socialist nations that have failed in their attempts to make society a level playing ground. Take health care; sure it's available for all and equally terrible for all. I have read so many nightmare stories of people who have been given death sentences in socialistic medical systems because the system doesn't recognize individual needs. It's so focused on the whole that the individual slips through the cracks of bureaucracy. I also have read stories where people get sicker or die from entering universal care hospitals. Health care woes are just one issue that has proven to be a burden of people with socialist or universal care.

The grass is not always greener on the other side as this article notes:

### Why does socialism always end up in oppression and poverty?
*(Speaking of Chavez and Venezuela)*

*... a training ground where workers could develop a socialist mindset, and thus an incubatorfor a more advanced stage of socialism. The governmentbelieved that working in an economic environment characterized by cooperation, sharing and joint democratic decision-making would instill socialist values and habits in them.*

*This was part of their program of building socialism from below, rather than imposing it from on high.*

-------

*So, the state took control of these cooperatives in the name of 'society.' Despite his promise that "we cannot resort to state capitalism, which would be the same perversion of the Soviet Union," that is exactly where Venezuelan socialism ended up. Much the same happened in the Soviet Union, Cuba, and China. The success of Cuban communism was based on the planned creation of a 'New Man' who would work selflessly for others and not for himself. When these 'New Men' failed to materialize, regular men were sent off to labor camps. They would emerge either 'New' men or dead men. The same went for the Soviet Union. The attempt to nationalize agriculture in the wake of the revolution lead to famine. As early as 1921, Lenin effectively gave up on the program and instituted the New Economic Policy. This saw a substantial return to the market economy in Russia and, through the mid-1920s, the economic situation of the Russian people improved. In China, the failure of collectivized agriculture starved millions to death. China's economic miracle only began when its farmers were allowed to sell some small share of their produce for profit.* [21]

Satan is a liar, and his ways always lead to misery. So back to what I wanted to share with you, my personal Voter Guide. This list is the foundation for how our family votes. It keeps us away from political drama as we focus on what really counts in an election. This list is to keep our eyes on what matters to our family, which is maintaining morality, religious freedom, and parental rights at a high priority.

*I Vote for*

*Righteousness!*

—Emma Sara

# Voter Guide

## Candidate Yes Vote

1. Protects parental rights in legislation.
   a. This includes NOT approving legislation that would strong-arm parents to go against their personal convictions.
   b. They will be a voice for our parental rights
   • "Gather me the people together, and I will make them hear my words, that they may learn to fear me all the days that they shall live upon the earth, and that they may teach their children. Deut. 4:10
2. Fights for religious liberty.
3. Works to keep the integrity of the Bill of Rights.
4. Favors Israel.
   • Blessed is he that blesseth thee and cursed is he that curseth thee. Num 24:9
5. Pro-life.
6. Pro sovereignty of the people.
   a. Capitalism allows us to shoot for the stars! You can start at the bottom and make it to the top! Think of self-made millionaires.
7. Supports our military and their families.
   a. My husband served our country, and I know what it feels like to live on meager paycheck!
8. Protects children's innocence.
   a. Fight to keep early education free of sexualization.

- Including- Curriculum causing gender confusion and inappropriate lessons for children.

**Candidate NO Vote:**

1. They believe that the government knows what's best for a child as in the "village" should decide.
2. Supports anti-family legislation
3. Supports a socialist form of government.
4. Favors unsafe societal legislation.
   a. Boys being able to use girls' bathrooms.
   b. Supports a women's choice to kill her child, especially late term abortion.
   c. Sexualization in school curriculums.
5. Dispassionate towards Israel.
6. Hostile to Biblical worldviews.
7. Hostile to the military that is protecting our nation.
8. Pro-abortion.

As I mentioned earlier, my list is not based upon a candidate's private lifestyle. I would love it if they had an upright life. Unfortunately, that hasn't often been the case with many people in office. I can think of people I have voted for in the past that had questionable lifestyle habits, but I was glad they stayed in line with our voting standard. As a citizen of this nation, we want people in office who will uphold moral standards. Of course, we pray for the salvation of those in office and that Yahweh would continually guide them.

*The king's heart is in the hand of the LORD, as the rivers of water: he turneth it whithersoever he will. Prov. 21:1*

In all things, go to prayers and ask Yahweh how He wants you to vote. Ask Him to give you understanding and insight.

# Prayer:

Yahweh, I come to you and ask that you reeducate my mind concerning political issues. Show me how to vote in every election. Reveal candidates to me that will uphold Biblical standards in our nation. Help me to vote according to the spirit rather than the flesh. Help our family to be united and undivided with our national vote too. Lead us to pathways of truth and revelation so we may serve you with confidence.

In Yeshua's name, amen.

# Call to Action

Mama, we just looked at our civil duty as Mothers of Change, now let's look at how we can step into our power as Warrior Queens.

## A Warrior Queen:

1. Protects her children from perversion.
2. Casts her literal vote to keep schools focused on academics and stands against sex-education for grade school students because it is unacceptable and damaging.
3. Protects her children from showing or viewing nakedness.
4. Takes action when her children are being bullied by advisors who are trying to make her children go against personal convictions.
5. Speaks up when she sees her child being put into dangerous situations. I reported that a library participant was looking at porn when my kids were at the library. The library didn't do anything initially until I involved local law enforcement who supported my concern. Because of our family's persistence, the library put up signs at each computer, now warning that it is a legal violation to view pornography on computers! Remember, never be afraid to speak up! Use your parental power to stand for your children.

6. She does not enable or support her kids to live contrary to the Word of God. Our kids may choose the wrong path, but we don't have to support it.
7. She does not let her guard down with her kid's peer group.
8. She is aware of the enemy's plan to disperse the spirit of androgyne/neutrality of gender, trying to morph God's creation.
9. She seeks God in all that she does.
10. She seeks to gain her husband's and kid's respect.
11. She honors God's boundaries, order, and structure for life.

If you are still unsure about agreeing to all these areas, please, consider at least seeking God about each of these topics.

**Remember**:
- It is loving to protect your kids from the schemes of the enemy.
- Enabling is not a form of love. Instead, it's practiced out of self-preservation. We use enabling to protect ourselves from doing hard things.
- Tough love is indeed love when practiced out of a desire to truly help someone break free from unhealthy behaviors.

Finally, remember you are a chain-breaker! You are a Mother of Change!

Now go out and change the world and start at home! Live the life you want to be remembered for!

Appendices

# Moms Q & A

Mama, I want to thank you for your desire to press into becoming a Mother of Change. I have counseled many moms over the years, and I know that you have questions. So, I wanted to include this Q & A with the most common question I have received over the years. I hope it provides encouragement and strategy for you!

**Question:** What if my kids are in a stage of rebellion?

**Answer:**

I had my season as a rebellious teenager. I was getting in trouble at school, hanging out with the wrong crowd, and I got kicked out of school for a semester. My mom was only twenty-eight, and she was frustrated with me because I violated her trust too many times. I can honestly say the best thing to happen to me at that stage was to get kicked out of school because I was no longer around a lousy peer group. I know my mom was praying, and she did not enable my bad behavior. She showed some tough love at times. She didn't allow me to make excuses for things I was doing. As a troubled teen, I can remember realizing that people I was trying to impress weren't true friends. I can remember getting in a fight once with two girls as my supposed two best friends just stood there and watched! My mom was livid. She tried to convince me they were not real friends. Finally, I acknowledged that I was trying to fit in with people who couldn't care less about my wellbeing. I couldn't lie to myself any longer at the age of sixteen. I started to see the cliques in school for what they were, and I decided that when I went back, I wasn't going to try and fit in. So, I made it a goal to excel in school because of my ability. I stopped caring about what people thought about me, and I shifted my attention to being the best I could be. I even went on to be the second runner in the Miss Teen Los Angeles Pageant!

So what does this have to do with raising troubled kids? It means hope for you, mama!

The answer lies in my turnaround. It has to do with a mindset change. We can't change what our kids think, but God can. He can change your kid's mindset. So my answer to you is to change what you have the power to and make that your initial focus. You can change you, the way you think, and the way you respond. Plus, you can change the lifestyle habits you have. Mama, I want to start with you. If your child is acting like a rebel, here is your strategy.

**Step 1:** If you need a breakthrough, it's time to fast and pray! For years I fasted for my kids on the same day of the week from month to month. I can attest that it not only kept my kids on track, but it also kept me on track. At some point, I slipped out of that practice, and I went through some real spiritual struggles personally, but my kids also had their share of personal failures. So, I am back at it. I am trying to get back on track with fasting throughout the month from 6 a.m. to 6 p.m. During the fast, I have water or herbal tea. You could also benefit from fasting from social media too on the same day, so you are more open to the voice of the Lord.

Keep a prayer journal, and make sure to note what you hear in prayer and record your victories no matter how small!

---

*However, this kind does not go out except by prayer and fasting. (Mathew 17:21)*

---

## Go to Yahweh and ask Him the following questions in Prayer:

1. Have I been an enabler to any bad habits my kid has?
2. Father, where have I turned a blind eye?
3. Is there any connection to my lifestyle choices that have negatively influenced my child?
4. Are there any generational bloodline curses that need to be broken in my life and my child's?

Father, how should I pray for my son/daughter?

After you hear from God in prayer, repent of anything He reveals to you that needs to be purged. Repent and make the necessary corrections. Remember, it is so important not to beat yourself up in this process. You can't change the past, but you can change the present. You may have failed in some areas, but that does not make you a failure. I have had many failures in my history as a mother. It comes along with the territory. Don't allow the enemy to use your mistakes to cause further damage. Your eyes will be open now, and you can claim the victory for your child because you have eyes to see and ears to hear the things of the Lord. Of course, you now have the MOC manual (this book) to glean from daily too.

**Step 2:** After you have gotten straight with yourself, you can move on to your child. This is when you press into your faith. I know this may be hard to believe, but remember, God loves your child more than you do. When I think back on my days of being out of control, first in my teen years and then for a few years in my young adult years, I can see the hand of Yahweh on my life. He protected me so many times. So, mama, believe and decree that He will not put more on your child than they can bare but remember, mama, you are part of the equation to provide a shield for them. Your prayers are an excellent defense! So don't let up, keep consistent, and never give up!

One time I heard Eric Thomas giving a message. He was addressing how to deal with kids who are in a self-destructive mode. He was talking about being concerned about his daughter going away to college. Parent fear is real, but we have to decide to trust God. We need to do our part, as I discussed through much of this book, and pair that with trusting God to protect our kids from others and sometimes themselves. So back to ET's message, he was sharing how he intercedes for his kids at 3 am and prays, "God bless them. God, whatever decisions they make, don't let it hurt them!" He said he was going through some concerns about his kid's staying safe, and his friend told him to put their name on the war board and put all their friends on it. Then ask God to take out every one of their friends that shouldn't be in their lives and keep everyone in their life that they need for growth. Then leave it all on the wall and don't think about it again. We are to warn them, true, but not fifty times, he said. This is where trust comes into play. If you need help hearing from God, make sure to join my family strategy sessions to be trained. A big part of teen success is about communicating with your kids, and I have extra resources to help you do just that, communicate better with them, see the back of the book for more details.

For now, make fasting a regular part of your weekly life.

Here is a **fasting prayer strategy** for your child:

1. Put your child's name, plus the names of their friends, into a journal and give your list over to God. Proclaim God to be their shield and protector.
2. Ask Yahweh to teach you how to hear the voice of the Holy Spirit clearly.
3. Ask for sin to be uncovered within your entire family so you can bring it to the light to repent and heal.
4. Pray for emotional stability and against fear.
5. Pray for peace despite your circumstances.
6. Ask that your child would get no satisfaction from living ungodly.
7. Pray that the Lord would surround them daily with divine appointments and good influences.
8. Ask the Lord to reveal secrets.
9. Finally, pray for the ability to use this manual to bring victory to your home. Use it to come into unity with the work of the Spirit throughout the pages. Don't forget to join our member's site to stay connected to other Mothers of Change! Support is available for you. You are not alone.

# A Call to Consecration

A month ago, I woke up with an urgency in my spirit that I knew was a message to share with the public on social medial. I decided to include it here for you because I think it's an important reminder to lead consecrated lives this year and every year of our lives.

I woke up and heard this multiple times...

This coming year will be the year to be CONSECRATED not sexy.

Sexy= sexually suggestive

Consecrated = to make or declare sacred.

I used to be a model, and I lived for the world, and my value was based upon my body. I believed the LIE from satan that I had to show my body to have worth, so I showed it off. I never left home without my favorite accessory, my cleavage.

As women, we have so much ability, BUT we sell ourselves short. We give guys a *free look* at the expense of our dignity. We are eye candy for free! Why? Why do we care what these men think?

Statistics show that over 80% of young men have a porn problem.

If those same men are checking you out for free don't kid yourself, they could care less about your wonderful personality + God given skill or your intelligence.

Why do we let satan lie to us? Why do we go against God's word and live according to the flesh if we call ourselves believers?

Right after I got that clear Word, I opened up my Bible app to today's devotion, " a) For whoever desires to save his/her life will lose it, b) but whoever loses his life for My sake will find it!

Losing our life= not living to please ourselves, but to magnify Yahweh.

Those who live according to the *flesh* have their minds set on what the *flesh* desires, but those who live in accordance with the Spirit have their minds set on what the Spirit desires. Roman's 8:5

*The mind governed by the flesh is death but the mind governed by the Spirit is life and peace. Rom 8:6*

*ALL that is in the world, the LUST of the flesh and the lust of the eyes and the boastful pride of life, is NOT from the Father, but is from the world. 1 John 2:16*

I have been pregnant twelve times. Yes, twelve.

I have 8 kids ages 1 to 20 and some seasons I still have four-pack stomach. My body looks like a 21-year-old at 45.

My flesh would desire to show the world.

But why? Why do I care if people are impressed with my body? I don't. I live to the Spirit. I stay fit for health and longevity. I stay fit for my husband and looking good for HIS eyes only.

Are you single? Cover up that body and WAIT for a gentleman who desires you because God has drawn him to you like he did Rachel to Jacob.

Life is too short to marry a guy who is a lust bucket! Y'all know how that turns out for marriage, right?

I am not writing to judge or make you feel shameful. Hey, I was in your shoes too. I was scandalous as a prodigal daughter and then as a newly committed Christian I was naive to think God didn't care if I showed my goods.

On the contrary, He does care because He is a GOOD father. You are His princess. His daughter. What good dad wants his daughter going out looking like a street walker? None that I know of.

Yes, I did look like one! See exhibit (A) taken when I was 21. (It was omitted for the book. It was a skintight tank dress, thigh length that was blurred out.)

Are you raising daughters? What kind of example are you providing for them?

What kinds of clothes are you buying them?

Who am I speaking to out there?

Pray and seek Yahweh on this matter. Let Him guide you.

# Consecrated Worship

Mama, we have covered so much ground in this family manual. You learned how to protect the gates of your home, and now we are going to talk about further consecration. Not only does God care about what we wear as His daughters, but He also cares about how we worship.

*God is Spirit, and those who worship Him must worship in spirit and truth. John 4:24*

Truth defined in the *Strong's Concordance* is divine truth revealed to man, and the *HELPS- WORD Study* defines it as the opposite of illusion. Why is this so important to understand? Because if you are trying to build a Godly legacy, this topic must be understood. This book is packed with stories about how the enemy comes to steal, kill and destroy, so let me give you one more illustration before I come to a close.

Yesterday during a family strategy session, the Lord put this phrase on my heart,

## "Golden Calf Movement."

As soon as it came to me, I could envision Israel dancing around the golden calf that they persuaded Aaron to make.

I could see them celebrating, dancing, singing, and calling out the name of Yahweh. Then my thoughts shifted to another scene that is common today. I saw conferences and mega-churches filled with yelling, fasting, praying, prophesying, and worked-up people dancing as popular church bands played. Then I heard it again, "The Golden calf movement." I understand there is a time to dance and sing before the Lord, so I am not saying that it is all ungodly. Just make sure that you survey your worship with a spirit of humility that doesn't make assumptions. Keep coming back to the Lord every step of the way for instructions on how to walk out your faith. There is a reason the scriptures says...

*All we like sheep have gone astray; we have turned everyone to his own way. (Isaiah 53:6)*

I care about your family too much not to include this warning for your family.

*Having a form of godliness but denying its power. And from such people turn away! For of this sort are those who creep into households and make captives of gullible women loaded down with sins, led away by various lusts, always learning and never able to come to the knowledge of the truth. (2 Tim. 3:7)*

Please, beware of this movement because not everyone that calls themselves children of God pleases Him with their lifestyle or worship.

*And the L*ORD *said unto Moses, I have seen this people, and, behold, it is a stiffnecked people: Now therefore let me alone, that my wrath may wax hot against them, and that I may consume them: and I will make of thee a great nation. Exodus 32:9-10*

It's easy to look religious, and it's easy to *look* consecrated, but it is the Lord and the Lord alone that sets our standard for worship. If we go against His decrees and commands, we have to deal with a Holy God who has shown us how He feels about unconsecrated worship.

Some people assume that just because they have the gift of prophesy or the gift of healing that God must be giving approval for their lifestyle, but do not be deceived.

*Not everyone who says to Me, 'Lord, Lord,' shall enter the kingdom of heaven, but he who does the will of My Father in heaven. Many will say to Me in that day, 'Lord, Lord, have we not prophesied in Your name, cast out demons in Your name, and done many wonders in Your name?' And then I will declare to them, 'I never knew you; depart from Me, you who practice lawlessness! (Mathew 7:21-23)*

For those who use religious acts as their badge of approval, beware!

*For false messiahs and false prophets will appear and perform signs and wonders to deceive, **if** possible, **even the elect.***
*(Mark 13:22)*

Again, spiritual works don't equate to a mark of approval. Remember, God is gracious to allow the rain to fall on the *just* and *unjust* (Mathew 5:45). In the marketplace, there are people who are opposed to Yahweh, yet appear to have great favor and receive many blessings. However, it *does not* validate their choice to oppose God. It only validates God's grace on humanity.

So I want you to be on your game for your family's sake. Worshipping Yahweh has been tainted from the very beginning. The '"Golden Calf Movement" was a term dropped in my lap that is connected with the Golden calf story, when Israel was just rescued from over four hundred years of slavery. They just experienced miracle after miracle. They saw the hand of Yahweh protect them, so they knew He was real and powerful. Three months out of Egypt, Yahweh declared to the children that if they keep His covenant they would be a peculiar people treasured above all people (Exod. 19:1,5). Then from verses 20 to 31, of Exodus 19, the people were given Yahweh's commandments on how to worship Him plus more. Even with all the precise instructions the people still failed greatly in obedience. After Moses delayed from coming back down the mountain while he was with Yahweh, the people became impatient and said to Aaron, Moses brother, "Make us a mighty ones which will go before us" (Exod 23:1). The short story is that Aaron made a golden calf for them with their gold jewelry, and he built an altar in front of it. Then he declared a feast to <u>Yahweh,</u> and the people did burnt offerings, they had a feast and they got "up to play" (Exod. 32:1-6). Did you get that? They were doing this worship service unto Yahweh. Here they were probably dancing and singing and feeling in one accord worshipping , meanwhile Yahweh was filled with wrath because of their disobedience to not make any graven images (Exod. 20:4).

Let's do a little rewind from earlier in this book.

- Music can be an idol. It can be worshipped. So, that means bands can be idols too! It is so easy for anyone of us to be led astray. It's totally possible to get sucked in. Our family got involved in what I am now calling the "Golden Calf Movement" for a couple of years. However, the Holy Spirit started to open my eyes because I began to pray, "Lord, help me not to be deceived, nor be a deceiver."

Part of the connection I made with this false movement is churches that teach that God breaks or bends laws out of love for us. If you hear this teaching move far from it! Beware! It's a doctrine of satan.

---

*But though we, or an angel from heaven, preach any other gospel unto you than that which we have preached unto you, let him be accursed. (Gal. 1:8)*

---

Keep watch:

1. **Spiritual works are not evidence of right standing with God.**
   a. Remember, in Mark 7:23, not all people who appear to have spiritual gifts will get into heaven. It is clear who will not, the workers of iniquity, defined as lawlessness.
2. **Be on guard for false teachings.**
   a. Read full books of the Bible, start to finish to know the Word.
3. **Be on guard for what the masses are doing.**
   a. Enter by the narrow gate; for wide *is* the gate and broad is the way that leads to destruction, and there are many who go in by it. Because *narrow* is the gate and *difficult* is the way which leads to life, and there are few who find it. Mathew 7:13-14

Once again mama, be on your guard for your household. Just because it's called worship, doesn't mean Yahweh receives it. Not all that is called holy is holy. The Mother of Change Movement is counterculture because we are a peculiar people, a chosen generation that have been called out of darkness into light and truth. Amen.

---

*But ye are a chosen generation, a royal priesthood, an holy nation, a peculiar people; that ye should shew forth the praises of him who hath called you out of darkness into his marvelous light. (1 Peter 2:9)*

---

Mama, you are equipped. You have everything you need to go forth and create change in this nation. You possess the right tools to raise Godly kids. Make sure to write down the first day that you took a step for change for your family. I know you won't keep this secret to raising a Godly generation to yourself. Thank you for spreading the word of the Mother of Change Movement because together we will take back our nation for Yahweh! Don't forget to stay connected in our Facebook group and sign-up for my Monthly Family Strategy Training, where the fire stays lit! I look forward to meeting you there! Remember...

## You are blessed!

You are a Mother of Change. You are a daughter of the Most High. You were called with a Holy calling to raise children who will be the salt and light of the earth. Your children will rise up and call you blessed, and your generations will be known for their allegiance to Yahweh.

You will eat the fat of the land and prosper all the days of your life. I declare all of this in the name of Yeshua/Jesus.

# MOC Prayer

Finally, here is a combo prayer/proclamation for you to repeat out loud whenever you need to POWER UP!

Jesus, thank you that you are guiding my heart, mind, and intellect. Thank you that my eyes are opened to the schemes of the enemy. Uproot any doctrines of man that I am holding onto in my heart.

Lord, help me to be led by your Spirit and not by popular opinion. Help me to submit my will to Yours in all circumstances.

Help me to uphold and live out Your Word. Strengthen me and give me a resolve not to be moved when people question my desire to serve You in all my ways.

I also thank You in advance that my kids will rise up and call me blessed! I thank You that they will choose to follow You all the days of their life and reverently fear you. Thank you that I will not be deceived, nor a deceiver.

Father continue to teach me how to walk fully in the mandate of being a Mother of Change for my kids and the good of my nation!

# Signs of Abuse

## Physical Signs of Abuse

- Direct physical signs of sexual abuse are not common. However, when physical signs are present, they may include bruising, bleeding, redness and bumps, or scabs around the mouth, genital, or anus. Urinary tract infections, sexually transmitted diseases, and abnormal vaginal or penile discharge are also warning signs.
- There are other indirect physical signs that include:
  o Persistent or recurring pain during urination or bowel movements
  o Wetting or soiling accidents unrelated to toilet training
  o Sexually transmitted diseases
  o Chronic stomach pain
  o Headaches

## Emotional Signs

- Emotional and behavioral signs or changes are more common and can include:
- Anxiety and depression
- Sleep disturbances, including nightmares or night terrors
- Change in eating habits
- Unusual fear of certain people or places; reluctance to be alone with a certain person
- Changes in mood that could including anger, aggressiveness towards parents, siblings, friends, pets

383

- Rebellion or withdrawal; runaway behavior
- Change in attitude towards school or academic performance, lack of interest in friends, sports, or other activities
- Unexplained or frequent health problems like headaches or stomach aches
- Poor self-esteem; avoidance of relationships
- Self-mutilation or change in body perception, like thinking of self or body as dirty or bad; suicidal thoughts
- Regression to previously outgrown behaviors, for example bedwetting or thumb sucking
- Abnormal sexual behaviors or knowledge of advanced sexual language and behaviors
- Too "perfect" behavior or overly compliant behavior

**FACT:** As many as 40% of children who are sexually abused are abused by older, or more powerful children.

• The younger the child victim, the more likely it is that the perpetrator is a juvenile. Juveniles are the offenders in 43% of assaults on children under age six. Of these offenders, 14% are under age 12.9

• Juveniles who commit sex offenses against other children are more likely than adult sex offenders to offend in groups, to offend at schools, and to have more male victims and younger victims.

• The number of youth coming to the attention of police for sex offenses increases sharply at age 12 and plateaus after age 14. Early adolescence is the peak age for youth offenses against younger children.

• A small number of juvenile offenders — one out of eight — are younger than age 12. Females constitute 7% of juveniles who commit sex offenses.

FACT: Child sexual abuse often takes place under specific, often surprising circumstances. It is helpful to know these circumstances because it allows for the development of strategies to avoid child sexual abuse.

• 81% of child sexual abuse incidents for all ages occur in one-perpetrator/one-child circumstances.

• 6 to 11-year-old children are most likely (23%) to be abused in multiple-victim circumstances.

• Most sexual abuse of children occurs in a residence, typically that of the victim or perpetrator – 84% for children under age 12, and 71% for children aged 12 to 17.

• Sexual assaults on children are most likely to occur at 8 a.m., 12 p.m. and between 3 and 4 p.m. For older children, aged 12 to 17, there is also a peak in assaults in the late evening hours.

• One in seven incidents of sexual assault perpetrated by juveniles occurs on school days in the after-school hours between 3 and 7 p.m., with a peak from 3 to 4 pm. [23]

(Signs of Abuse was used with permission from Darkness to Light https://www.d2l.or)

# References

1. www.smart.gov/SOMAPI/sec1/ch3_typology.html
2. records.txdps.state.tx.us/SexOffenderRegistry/Search/Rapsheet?Sid=08184646
3. www.cdc.gov/vitalsigns/suicide/index.html
4. www.d2l.org/the-issue/prevalence/
5. www.d2l.org/wp-content/uploads/2017/01/Statistics_2_Perpetrators.pdf
6. www.fatherhood.org/fatherhood-data-statistics
7. www.washingtonexaminer.com/opinion/mother-absence-matters-just-as-much-as-father-absence
8. www.attachment.org/product/when-love-is-not-enough-a-guide-to-parenting-children-with-rad/
9. www.apa.org/news/press/releases/2017/08/pornography-exposure
10. www.foxnews.com/us/human-trafficking-in-america-among-worst-in-world-report
11. https://www.nbcnews.com/news/us-news/duty-deputy-who-helped-thwart-florida-kidnapping-was-shock-n588326
12. Health Education Framework, Section 1166 & 1167
13. https://www.cnsnews.com/news/article/msnbc-we-have-break-through-idea-kids-belong-their-parents
14. https://www.americanexperiment.org/2019/03/socialism-always-end-oppression-poverty/

15. (https://www.news5cleveland.com/news/state/suicide-is-now-the-leading-cause-of-death-for-children-ages-10-to-14-in-ohio)
16. https://wfww.washingtonpost.com/news/worldviews/wp/2015/04/14/map-these-are-the-worlds-least-religious-countries/
17. https://www.bbc.com/news/world-europe-14038419
18. https://www.washingtonpost.com/context/transitional-k-3-sex-gender-guidelines/5ba0fb8c-95f0-4183-b1af-2d990ff05671/
19. (http://www.d2l.org/wp-content/uploads/2017/01/all_statistics_20150619.pdf)
20. (https://www.researchgate.net/publication/270692132_The_Devil_Is_Red_Socialist_Satanism_in_the_Nineteenth_Century)
21. ( https://en.wikipedia.org/wiki/Radical_left)
22. (https://www.americanexperiment.org/2019/03/socialism-always-end-oppression-poverty/)
23. http://www.d2l.org/wp-content/uploads/2017/01/all_statistics_20150619.pdf
24. (Generation XXX: Pornography Acceptance and Use Among Emerging Adults. Journal of Adolescent Research V.23 2008)

# Educational Resources

### Xtreme Change University
https://www.xtremechangeuniversity.com/

Experience an extreme family makeover on Xtreme Change University, our online learning platform created to help your family grow!

### Khan Academy
https://www.khanacademy.org/

Khan Academy is a non-profit educational organization created in 2008 by Salman Khan to create online tools that help educate students. The organization produces short lessons in the form of videos. Its website also includes supplementary practice exercises and materials for educators

My kids have been using Khan for years. It's free and offers top-notch academics.

## Apex4Kids

Apex4Kids programs help kids learn to manage their emotions and stress by offering solutions and key techniques to shift from a reactive mindset to a responsible mindset, helping kids face life and challenges with greater balance and ease.

My kids all love Apex4Kids. It has taught them about being entrepreneurs and it's great for character development.

Make sure to use our affiliate link (no extra cost to you) http://bit.ly/2SQjnhU

# This is my story

Use this section to create your NEW family narrative. Write down what you want your family to be known for. Write out your dream for your family legacy. Write it out present tense, not future tense. Write it in now words as if you are already living the dream.

Date _____

_____

_____

_____

_____

_____

_____

_____

# Has the Lord given you promises?

Write them down and believe they will come to pass.

_____

_____

_____

_____

_____

_____

_____

# My Scriptures

Choose two verses that will be your family scriptures for life and write them out. For example: Our chapter is Isaiah 58. You can choose a passage or a chapter.

_____

_____

_____

_____

_____

_____

_____

_____

_____

# Family goals

1. _____
2. _____
3. _____
4. _____
5. _____
6. _____
7. _____
8. _____
9. _____
10. _____
11. _____
12. _____
13. _____

Where there is no vision, the people perish.
Prov. 29:18

# About the Author

EmmaSara is a woman of God who speaks and teaches truth. She is also a behavior consultant who specializes in the art of communication. As a speaker and certified behavior coach, she empowers moms to break free from broken generational mindsets to flourish in faith, family, and finance to find fulfillment in motherhood. When she is not speaking and doing workshops, she is studying the Word and raising her eight kids to be entrepreneurs.

EmmaSara is also the founder of the Mother of Change Movement and Kidz of Change. Seven of her children are entrepreneurs, plus she has a toddler who is a joy.

A proud mama moment.

# About the Kids

At the age of thirteen, Bijou was awarded a weekend scholarship for film workshops for her film entry into the San Antonio Christian Film Festival. At the age of twenty-one she is now the COO for McMillion & Co. LLC. She was also a lead administrative assistant for a multi-million-dollar company and their book editor. She is also the founder and filmmaker for Psalm Project Films. You can find her films on YouTube.

Nile was born to fly. At the age of seventeen he took EmmaSara flying to celebrate their shared birthday. It was one the proudest day of EmmaSara's life. At the age of nine-teen he bought his second plane and his first truck cash. Nile is also the youngest engineer working at a west Texas space facility. For fun and extra cash, he is also a licensed drone pilot.

When Davae was small her nickname was "money bags," because she had the gift of entrepreneurship at a young age. Sixteen was a milestone age for her. She wrote her first book. She also became one of the youngest alumnae at Liberty University. Soon after she got a job with a multi-million-dollar company where she was the head of creatives. She is now a musician and she is working to release singles this year.

At the age of thirteen, Von-Kensington became one the youngest people to be certified by AWS as an Amazon Web Services Cloud Practitioner which has six-figure starting salary. At fourteen is a co-found of Kidz of Change and he is known as the The Teen Tech Tutor. He now teaches monthly courses on Xtreme Change University.

When Remington was about six, he had a dream that he would be a pastor to a walking church. At the age of ten became known as the "Pastor" for the Kidz of Change Facebook community. He loves to study scripture and make it exciting for kids to learn and understand. Remington is planning on releasing a series of bible memorization videos this year!

Van-Houston is something like child a prodigy. At the age of two he taught himself how to read two and three letter words. By the age of three he could read out of the KJV bible. By the age of seven he was assessed by a Harvard graduate and Organic Chemistry tutor. The tutor was so impressed he said, "Van-Houston should be put on T.V. and enrolled into college to show other students that a kid can do it." try courses."

Meet Brighton! At the age of four he had an idea for a book. His big sisters had him speak the whole story line and recorded him. They helped him to publish his book allowing him to become the youngest American author in decades. He is currently working on his next business plan to go along with his book

This is Princeton. He is the baby in the family. He is still working on speaking clearly, but he is bright and interested in life. He loves to be independent and play with the family.

Join my *Membership* Group at www.EmmaSara.com for accountability, support and impacting resources created just for you.

Thank you for reading this book. I am praying your mom-life will never be the same again! I believe your family life will be more intentional and focused on glorifying God. If you felt inspired to grow, I would love it if you left your book review on Amazon. Let your story impact others; leave your mark mama!

Also, I would like to invite you to join the...

## Mother of Change Facebook Group

A community of like-minded moms who are motivated to build a godly family legacy. **@MotherofChangeGroup**

# Stay Connected

Don't forget **to POST photos** with your MOC Book. Use the hashtag **#MotherofChange** so I can send some love and prayers your way! To work with me or to book me to speak go to: **www.EmmaSara.com**

**Follow me on**  **@EmmaSara**

@EmmaSara_McMillion

EmmaSara.McMillion

EmmaSara McMillion

www.EmmaSara.com

## Passion. Purpose. Time Management.

Finding your calling. Fine-tuning your life.

This book is great for women of all ages.
It is never too early or late to find your calling.
Enjoy it for self or use it in a group study.

### Available on

Amazon

## Fearless Birth
### Empowered | Trauma-Free

Learn the secret to having a beautiful trauma-free birth.
Yes, it is possible to have a pain-free birth!
This book makes a great gift!

### Available on

*Amazon*

## She Writes Art
Beautiful truth portrayed in art + words.

By Davae McMillion (EmmaSara's daughter)
Consider it an invitation to discover your personal worth.
Perfect for teens and women young at heart.
Even little girls love it as a color book.

Available on

*Amazon*

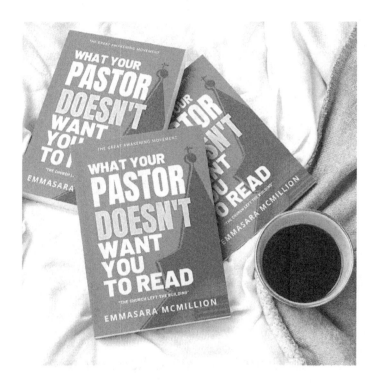

## What Your Pastor Doesn't Want You to Read
### The Church Left The Building

One of the most important books of the decade.
The line has been drawn in the sand,
which side will you choose?

### Available on

*Amazon*

## Brighton's Dino Adventures
A (not so) true story

By Brighton McMillion the youngest author in America!

A must read for any kid who loves dinos! Not only do kids love the images, but they also think it's funny too. Kids love to laugh when they read this story. Parents will love that it also teaches good character. Every child should be taught how to persevere, and this book does just that.

### Available on

*Amazon*

You are a

# Mother of Change!

The future is in your hands.

Made in the USA
Coppell, TX
20 January 2021